CALIFORNIA CULINARY ACADEMY

Chicken & Other Poultry

JULIE RENAUD
JANE HORN
Writers

SALLY W. SMITH
Editor

LINDA HINRICHS
CAROL KRAMER
Designers

BOB MONTESCLAROS
Photographer

DOUG WARNE
Food Stylist

SUZANNE P. McELWEE
CARLA TAVARES
Photographic Stylists

Danielle Walker *(top)* is chairman of the board and founder of the California Culinary Academy. **Julie Renaud** *(bottom left)* is a cook, caterer, and private cooking instructor trained in the classical European tradition. Experienced in a number of food-related areas, including recipe development and testing, consulting, and gourmet-food retailing, she currently teaches in the Culinary Arts Department at Contra Costa College in San Pablo, California. **Jane Horn** *(bottom right)*, a free-lance food editor and writer, has a bachelor's degree in home economics from Cornell University and a master's degree in communications from Stanford University. Her experience in writing and editing on the subject of food includes articles for newspapers and magazines, a weekly newspaper column, and six cookbooks.

The California Culinary Academy Among the forefront of American institutions leading the culinary renaissance in this country, the California Culinary Academy in San Francisco has gained a reputation as one of the most outstanding professional chef training schools in the world. With a teaching staff recruited from the best restaurants of Western Europe, the California Culinary Academy educates students from around the world in the preparation of classical cuisine. The recipes in this book were created in consultation with the chefs of the California Culinary Academy. For information about the Academy, write the Office of the Dean, California Culinary Academy, 625 Polk St., San Francisco, CA 94102.

Front Cover

Poussins are very young and tender chickens, usually under six weeks of age and weighing about 1 pound—enough to serve one or two people. Shown on the cover, roasted poussins (see page 20) served with rice and assorted fresh vegetables.

Title Page

For Basil-Stuffed Breasts (see page 19), an aromatic mixture of fresh basil, garlic, olive oil, and bread crumbs is inserted under the skin of boned chicken breast halves, which are then formed into a roll and roasted until crisp and golden brown.

Back Cover

Upper left: Leeks, carrots, potatoes, onions, garlic, and herbs are just some of the ingredients that go into a rich veal stock.

Upper right: Tempura Chicken (see page 66)—crisp on the outside, flavorful and juicy inside—is a quickly prepared, succulent entrée.

Lower left: Pheasant, marinated in a garlicky red-wine mixture, is cooked with green onions in parchment in a clay pot (see page 27). This method keeps the bird moist; the cooking juices become the base for a tangy sauce.

Lower right: Four Cornish game hens are arranged artfully on a platter with baby carrots and green beans. Among the lessons to be learned from professional chefs is that the way food is presented is just as important as how it tastes.

Contributors

Calligrapher
Chuck Wertman

Recipe Consultants
Craig Bryars
Marta Cormier
Suzanne Criaris
Bonnie McClean
Elizabeth Renaud
Tom and Sue Renaud

Additional Photographers
Michael Lamotte, back cover, upper left and lower right
Laurie Black, Academy photography
Fischella, photograph of Danielle Walker
Rich Powers, assistant

Additional Food Stylists
Amy Nathan, back cover, upper left and lower right
Jeff Van Hanswyk, at The Academy

Editorial Staff
Stephen McElroy
Don Mosley
Catherine Pearsall
Rebecca Pepper

Art and Production Staff
Deborah Cowder
Lezlly Freier
Kate O'Keeffe
Anne Pederson
Bill Yusavage

Lithographed in U.S.A. by
Webcrafters, Inc.

The California Culinary Academy series is produced by the staff of Ortho Information Services.

Publisher
Robert L. Iacopi

Production Director
Ernie S. Tasaki

Series Managing Editor
Sally W. Smith

Photographic Director
Alan Copeland .

Address all inquiries to:
Ortho Information Services
Chevron Chemical Company
Consumer Products Division
575 Market Street
San Francisco, CA 94105
Copyright © 1985
Chevron Chemical Company
All rights reserved under international and Pan-American copyright conventions.

1 2 3 4 5 6 7 8 9
85 86 87 88 89 90

ISBN 0-89721-056-5

Library of Congress Catalog Card Number 85-072800

Chevron Chemical Company
575 Market Street, San Francisco, CA 94105

C O N T E N T S

Chicken & Other Poultry

An array of eggs makes a fitting opening to a treasure trove of poultry cooking techniques and recipes. For information on eggs, see page 7.

A Cook's Guide to Poultry

P oultry," wrote Brillat-Savarin
in 1825, "is for the cook what
a canvas is for a painter." Its mild
flavor and almost universal availability
have made it central to the cuisines
of the world. The more than 175 recipes in
this book—dependable and easy-to-follow
variations of classics as well as exciting
new dishes—showcase this versatile and
adaptable food. In addition to this
wealth of reliable and tempting recipes,
each chapter is a complete lesson
on one type of cooking, giving you all
the skills you'll need to cook poultry
successfully, by whatever
method you prefer.

POULTRY: ECONOMICAL, VERSATILE, AND POPULAR

Since the jungle ancestors of today's domestic fowl first pecked and scratched their way around Southwestern Asia thousands of years ago, poultry has traveled the globe to become perhaps our most popular source of animal protein. It is certainly the most versatile. Poultry has always held an honored place on the American table, and has played an important economic role as well. Through the early part of this century, young and tender chickens were valued as much for their usefulness as breeders and egg producers as they were for food. In most households, a chicken dinner was a luxury reserved for special occasions, and then it was generally an old hen past its prime, rendered succulent and flavorful only by hours of slow cooking in the stew pot. Roast or fried chicken was commonplace only in the homes of the wealthy. Since the late 1940s, however, technological advances and more efficient production have made chicken available and affordable to almost every American family for any occasion.

Turkey is also an American favorite. It was the Indians who introduced early settlers to this native bird, which was part of the first Thanksgiving feast. Americans were so fond of turkey that Ben Franklin proposed that this "true original native of America" be our national bird instead of the eagle, which he dismissed as a "bird of bad moral character." The turkey we enjoy today is actually a cross between Franklin's wild turkey and a domesticated variety brought to this country from Europe by colonists.

Once eaten mainly at Thanksgiving and Christmas, it is now enjoyed all year. In fact, these days, more turkey is sold during the first three quarters of the year than in November and December.

Americans are eating more poultry than ever before. Between 1960 and 1980, per capita consumption of chicken and turkey almost doubled, while prices remained attractively low. If this trend continues, industry experts project that by the year 2000 poultry will be America's most popular meat.

Consumers are buying more poultry because it offers convenience, value, and nutrition as well as good taste. Chicken and turkey are excellent, economical sources of high-quality protein, low in fat and calories, and are available in a variety of forms—whole, cut up, ground, formed into roasts, or processed into cold cuts.

HOW TO SELECT POULTRY

Poultry is available both fresh and frozen. Ideally fresh poultry should be purchased and cooked within two to three days after slaughter; with each day, there are subtle changes in the texture and flavor of the flesh that result in a loss of quality, until finally the meat becomes unfit to eat. Sometimes it is difficult to tell how fresh a bird is, but there are certain indicators that can make the guess a little more educated.

Fresh poultry will have no off odor or off color, it will have a relatively dry surface, and if it's packaged, there will be no accumulated liquid on the tray. Prepackaged fresh poultry often has a "sell-by" date stamped on the label. This date, seven days after the bird was processed, is the cutoff date for sale only. As long as the bird is refrigerated at cold temperatures (28° F to 32° F), it will

keep several more days. For unwrapped poultry on display, ask the butcher how fresh it is and how soon it should be cooked.

When fresh poultry is not available, or if it must be purchased well before it is cooked, commercially frozen poultry is an acceptable alternative. Be alert, however, to signs of less-than-ideal condition. Do not buy a torn package; the exposed flesh will dry out and deteriorate. Avoid packages that contain frozen liquid, which indicates that the bird has been thawed and refrozen, with a considerable loss of quality.

GOVERNMENT INSPECTION AND GRADING

Almost all poultry in the United States is inspected for wholesomeness by either the federal or the state government. The United States Department of Agriculture's mark of inspection indicates that the poultry is safe to eat and is truthfully labeled. This round mark appears on all packaged or frozen poultry, but may not appear on other types of bird.

Besides being inspected, chicken, turkey, duck, and goose may also be graded for quality according to USDA guidelines. Grading is a voluntary

service provided by the federal government for a fee and is an evaluation of appearance only, not tenderness, which is related to age. Grade A birds, the best quality, will be plump, meaty, and well formed, without any defects such as tears or bruises on the skin or flesh. Grades B and C are of lesser quality and almost never offered for sale. Graded poultry may carry a shield stamped on the wrapper, the label, a wing tag or metal wing clip, the giblet wrap, or an insert, often in combination with the inspection mark and product class (such as broiler or fryer).

WHICH BIRD TO BUY?

At the market, poultry is grouped by species, such as chicken, turkey, or duck, and by class—for example, broilers, fryers, or roasters. Within each class birds may be grouped by physical characteristics, primarily age, which in turn determine the cooking method.

Younger birds are more tender and are best suited for roasting, baking, grilling, sautéing, and frying. The terms to look for are: for chickens, *Rock Cornish game hen, broiler, fryer, roaster,* and *capon;* for turkeys, *young turkey, fryer-roaster, young hen,* or *young tom;* for ducks, *duckling, young duckling, broiler* or *fryer duckling,* or *roaster duckling;* for goose, *young goose; squab* is a young pigeon.

Older birds need long, slow cooking with moist heat to break down tough connective tissue, so they should be used in stews, braises, and fricassees, or for stock. The terms to look for are: for chickens, *mature chicken, hen, fowl, baking,* or *stewing chicken;* for turkeys, *mature turkey, yearling turkey,* or *old turkey (hen* or *tom);* for ducks and geese, *mature* or *old.*

ABOUT EGGS

Western cuisine is dependent on the egg. It is eaten for itself in myriad forms; it adds flavor, moisture, and leavening to breads, cakes, and other baked dishes; it forms the base for sauces, functioning as a thickener, binder, and flavoring agent.

In choosing eggs, look first for the USDA grade. The top grades are AA and A, with the latter most commonly available in the market. The yolks of these eggs should form a high dome, the whites should be thick and firm, and the shells should be free from blemishes and cracks. Eggs are also classed by size, which is determined by weight per dozen eggs. Most recipes assume the use of large eggs. Don't concern yourself with shell color; it is determined by the breed of hen, and has no relationship to the flavor or quality of the egg.

As a rule, buy eggs as fresh as possible. The only exception is in selecting eggs to be hard-cooked; older eggs will be easier to peel. To test an egg for freshness, place it in a bowl of cold water. A fresh egg will lie on the bottom; an older egg will float to some degree. Discard any egg that rises to the surface of the water. Refrigerate eggs promptly after purchase and keep cold.

NO-FAIL HARD-COOKED EGGS

One of the tests of a cook is that he or she be able to "boil an egg." Here's a tried-and-true method.

Fill a pan with enough cold water to cover eggs by 1 inch. Add 2 teaspoons salt per quart of water; bring the water to a boil. Lower eggs (the oldest in your refrigerator) into boiling water with a slotted spoon. Bring water to a simmer, with bubbles that barely break on the surface. Simmer, uncovered, 10 minutes. Immediately plunge eggs into cold water or set under cold running water (the eggs will be easier to peel and won't develop a green ring around the yolk). Cool 1 hour in cold water.

Hard-cooked eggs are easier to peel when they're warm. Peel by tapping all around the shell with a knife to form a network of cracks. Peel shell away under cold running water. Use shelled eggs immediately or store in a bowl of cold salted water in the refrigerator up to two weeks.

DEVILED EGGS

> 6 *hard-cooked eggs, peeled and halved lengthwise*
> 3 *tablespoons mayonnaise*
> 1 *tablespoon Dijon mustard*
> ⅛ *teaspoon salt*
> *Paprika*

1. With a small spoon lift egg yolks out of whites. Place yolks in small bowl.

2. Add mayonnaise, mustard, and salt to egg yolks; mix well with a fork to make a very smooth paste. Adjust seasonings, if necessary.

3. Arrange egg-white halves on a serving platter. Mound some of yolk mixture into each one and sprinkle with paprika. Serve immediately or store, covered, in refrigerator until ready to use.

Makes 1 dozen deviled eggs.

HOW MUCH TO BUY

Bird	Amount
Poussin	½ to 1 per person
Rock Cornish game hens	½ to 1 per person
Other chickens	
with bones	about ½ lb per serving
without bones	about 4–6 oz per serving
As other than a main course	2 oz per serving
To yield 1 cup diced cooked meat	¾ lb
Turkey	
under 12 lbs	¾ lb per serving
over 12 lbs	½ lb per serving
with leftovers	1 to 2 lbs per serving
Duck	4- to 4½-lb bird serves 2
Goose	12- to 14-lb bird serves 12 to 14
Pheasant	2-lb bird serves 2 to 3
Squab	1 to 2 per person as a first course
Quail	2 to 3 per person as a first course

To make the choice, then, you either buy the bird that is appropriate for the recipe or cooking method you intend to use, or you adapt your cooking plan to suit the bird that catches your eye. Sometimes the occasion will dictate the choice: For a special celebration, costly pheasant may be preferable to the economical but more commonly eaten chicken.

Convenience has also become increasingly important. Sales of cut-up poultry and specialty packages—turkey drumsticks or boned chicken breasts, for instance—have risen at a faster rate over the past 25 years than sales of whole birds. Today's cook seems to prefer ready-to-cook poultry.

BUYING CHICKEN

According to an industry survey, chicken is eaten on a regular basis in almost every household, at least weekly in a majority of families. Chicken is available ready-to-cook in a variety of forms: whole, halves, quarters, and parts (breasts, drumsticks, thighs, wings, and wing drummettes—the meaty section of the wing). When buying fresh chicken, follow the guidelines for fresh poultry given on pages 6 and 7. Depending on where you live, chicken may be either white or yellow; color is determined by feed and regional preference, and is not an indicator of quality or wholesomeness.

Select the class of chicken that is appropriate to your needs (see "Poultry Primer," opposite page). For variety, consider: *poussin*, a delicately flavored, very young chicken that will serve one or two people; *Rock Cornish game hen*, a small hybrid developed by crossing a Plymouth Rock hen and a Cornish Game cock, wonderful stuffed, and just right for one or two people; *capon*, a desexed male chicken so succulent, tender, and meaty that it is perhaps the ideal bird for roasting.

Fresh and frozen chicken is in the market all year. Poussin, Rock Cornish game hens, and capons may be either fresh or frozen, depending on availability.

BUYING TURKEY

Benjamin Franklin's "respectable" bird is no longer a one-season food. Fresh whole turkeys, as well as turkey parts and processed turkey products, are now widely available on a year-round basis. The forms in which turkey, fresh or frozen, is available include: whole birds; halves or quarters; boneless roasts; bone-in or boneless whole, halved, or sliced breasts; fillets; drumsticks; wings; drummettes; thighs; and ground turkey.

Convenience options include prebasted birds, injected with natural ingredients intended to keep the bird moist (properly roasted, a bird will be moist and juicy without prebasting, however); frozen stuffed birds; and pop-up or retractable thermometers that activate when the bird has heated to a preset temperature.

Most turkeys are marketed as "Young Turkeys," which means 14 to 22 weeks old, either female or male (see "Poultry Primer," opposite). Despite a long-held belief to the contrary, the only difference between a hen and a tom is their size; their quality is the same. Hens are smaller—7 to 15 pounds; toms are 15 to more than 25 pounds. Fryer-roaster turkeys are very young birds, weighing 4 to 8 pounds.

POULTRY PRIMER

Kind	Age	Size	Preparation
Chicken			
Poussin	under 6 weeks	1 lb	broil, roast, grill, sauté
Rock Cornish game hen	4 to 5 weeks	1 to 1½ lbs	broil, roast, grill, sauté
Broiler	7 to 9 weeks	1½ to 2 lbs	broil, roast, grill, sauté
Fryer	9 to 12 weeks	3 to 4 lbs	broil, roast, grill, fry
Roaster	10 to 20 weeks	over 5 lbs	roast, fry, stew, braise
Capon	16 to 20 weeks	6 to 9 lbs	roast
Stewing chicken	over 10 months	4 to 6 lbs	stew, braise, make broth
Turkey			
Fryer-roaster (whole)	under 16 weeks	4 to 8 lbs	roast
Young turkey (whole):			
hen	14 to 22 weeks	7 to 15 lbs	roast
tom	14 to 22 weeks	15 to 25-plus lbs	roast
Mature turkey	over 15 months	12 to 25 lbs	stew, make broth
Other			
Duckling	8 to 16 weeks	3 to 5½ lbs	broil, roast
Young goose	over 6 months	4 to 14 lbs	roast
Pheasant	6 weeks	2 to 3 lbs	roast, bake
Squab	under 6 weeks	¾ lb	broil, roast, grill, sauté
Quail	under 6 weeks	¼ to ½ lb	broil, roast, grill, sauté

BUYING OTHER BIRDS

Domesticated (commercially raised) poultry and game birds such as duck, goose, squab, and quail can be purchased fresh or frozen throughout the year. Pheasant is only available seasonally, usually September through February. Ordering in advance will give you a greater choice. Most butchers will be able to accommodate special orders with two or three days' notice.

HOW TO GET THE MOST FOR YOUR MONEY

Generally, the least expensive poultry is that which has had the least amount of processing. Whole birds are cheaper per pound than those cut up and sold in parts; boned poultry costs more than that with the bone in. However, the best value may not be the poultry with the lowest cost per pound. Also to be taken into account is the yield, or number of servings per pound. A boneless turkey roast may be more expensive per pound than a whole turkey, but it is totally edible. It will yield more servings per pound than a whole bird, so the cost per serving will be lower. The USDA calculates the percentage of edible meat in various poultry cuts as follows: whole or cut up, 51 percent; legs and thighs, 53 percent; breasts, 63 percent; wings, 50 percent; and backs, 42 percent.

HANDLING AND STORING POULTRY SAFELY

Fresh poultry is extremely perishable. It should be stored in the coldest part of the refrigerator and used as soon as possible. Refrigerating fresh poultry does not kill food-spoilage organisms; it only slows their growth. If stored at about 40° F, the usual setting for most refrigerators, poultry should be cooked and eaten within one to two days of purchase. If stored at a temperature several degrees lower, it can be refrigerated another one or two days before signs of spoilage become noticeable. Spoiled meat will have a definite off odor and a slimy surface. Discard any meat that is of questionable freshness.

Prepackaged poultry can be left in its tray-pack, with transparent wrapping intact, for refrigerator storage. The wrapping protects it from contamination that may result from handling, and prevents moisture loss. If the wrapping is torn, or if it is wrapped in butcher's paper, remove the wrapping, set the poultry on a plate, and cover it with waxed paper.

Cooked poultry can be refrigerated for three or four days, well wrapped to keep it from drying out. For longer storage, freeze it. Cooked poultry in broth or gravy should be refrigerated only one or two days. Do not cool cooked poultry at room temperature (about 70° F). At between 60° F and 125° F potentially toxic organisms flourish. Four hours is the *most* time raw or cooked poultry can safely be left at room temperature. Chilling after two hours ensures a greater margin of safety.

FREEZING POULTRY

If you know in advance that you are buying for your freezer, consider commercially frozen products. They are frozen immediately after slaughter and packaged in special wrap. Assuming good handling by the processor and retailer, and proper cooking at home, there will be no noticeable loss of quality.

To minimize loss of flavor and deterioration of texture, frozen poultry should be kept at 0° F or lower. If you are using a refrigerator freezer compartment, check its temperature. Many cannot maintain a consistent 0° F, which means a faster loss of frozen-food quality.

Wrap poultry in heavy-duty aluminum foil or moisture/vapor-resistant wrap, such as freezer paper or film. Polyethylene freezer bags are another option. Wrap or bag meat airtight and seal well to maintain quality and prevent freezer burn—dry, white patches that make meat tough and tasteless. Label packages with contents, amount, and date. Use older items first. When you freeze several parts in the same package, put a piece of freezer wrap between the pieces so they will separate more easily when thawing. Poultry may be frozen up to one year, depending on the type of poultry and whether it is cooked or uncooked. Use "Timetable for Freezing Poultry" (at left) as a guide.

To Thaw Frozen Poultry

Poultry should be thawed until pliable and then refrigerated or cooked immediately; do not let thawed poultry sit at room temperature for more than four hours.

There are several methods of thawing poultry. The choice depends on the time available. Regardless of method, poultry must be kept cold while thawing.

The safest method is to thaw wrapped, frozen poultry on a tray in the refrigerator. For a large turkey, allow about three days; allow about one to two days for smaller birds. Or, calculate about 24 hours' thawing time per 5 pounds of frozen bird. Frozen parts will thaw in one day.

For quicker thawing, thaw in waterproof, completely sealed wrap under *cold* running water, or in cold water that is changed frequently to maintain a consistent temperature. A 5- to 9-pound bird will thaw this way in 4 to 6 hours. A bird over 9 pounds needs 8 to 12 hours.

Thaw poultry at room temperature *only* if you are able to carefully monitor the thawing process, because

bacteria that can cause food poisoning grow rapidly at this temperature. To thaw a turkey, place the unwrapped frozen bird in a double-walled brown bag or several thicknesses of newspaper. The paper keeps the bird's surface cold while the interior thaws. Frozen small birds and frozen poultry parts can be thawed in their wrapping. Refrigerate or cook the poultry as soon as possible.

A FINAL CAUTION

Because raw poultry may carry potentially harmful organisms, it's important to be particularly careful when handling it. Always wash hands, preparation surfaces (counters and chopping boards), and utensils in hot, soapy water before and after coming in contact with raw poultry. Thoroughly wash and dry raw poultry before using.

IN THE KITCHEN

Although it is always fun to buy culinary paraphernalia, most cooks function extremely well with a basic collection of well-chosen, high-quality equipment that suits their particular needs, and a pantry outfitted to complement their cooking style. The following is a checklist of equipment (in addition to basics such as liquid and dry measures and measuring spoons) and ingredients that would be helpful to have on hand for preparing the recipes in this book or any poultry recipes.

EQUIPMENT

Chinois; fat separator; instant-read meat thermometer; candy/frying thermometer; polyethylene cutting boards; knives (high quality, carbon steel or high-carbon stainless steel)— 8- to 10-inch chef's knife, boning knife, paring knife, chef's fork; sharpening steel; kitchen shears;

Among the equipment useful for cooking poultry are (from left rear): instant-read meat thermometer (on cutting board); tightly woven cheesecloth and kitchen parchment (at rear); chinois (upside down, in center). Arrayed in front are: vegetable peeler, kitchen shears, pastry brush, poultry shears, bulb baster, wooden spoon, meat pounder, citrus zester, melon baller, chef's fork, chef's knives, sharpening steel, whisks, metal spatula, and measuring spoons.

poultry shears; slotted spoon; offset spatula; kitchen string; good-quality cheesecloth (tight weave); flour cloth; kitchen parchment; meat pounder; saucepans (heavy bottomed, with tight-fitting lids, and of a material that is a good heat conductor)—1-quart, 3-quart, Dutch oven, 8-quart stockpot; wok, roasting pan and rack; 12-inch skillet and 4-quart sauté pan (same criteria as for saucepans); casseroles and baking dishes—9- by 13-inch shallow baking dish, 9- by 9-inch baking dish, deep ovenproof casseroles with lids; bulb baster; basting brushes; clay pot baker; baking sheets and cooling racks; vertical roaster.

INGREDIENTS

Canned chicken stock (various sizes); fresh parsley, dried thyme, bay leaves for bouquet garni; dry bread crumbs; unsalted and salted butter; milk; whipping cream; half-and-half; sour cream or crème fraîche; eggs; vegetable shortening; flour; garlic; cooking oils—olive, vegetable, walnut, grapeseed, sesame, peanut; onions; shallots; pasta; rice; potatoes; sugar; cornstarch; vinegars—sherry, white, cider, tarragon, rice wine; soy sauce; ginger; mayonnaise; mustards; tomato paste and canned whole tomatoes; wines and liqueurs—white and red wine, vermouth, Marsala, Madeira, pale dry sherry; cheese—Parmesan, jack, sharp Cheddar; good-quality herbs and spices, including salt, black and white pepper, Hungarian paprika, and curry powder; juniper berries; citrus fruit—lemon, orange; vegetables—celery, carrots, and onion for mirepoix, mushrooms; fresh basil; pesto sauce.

PREPARING POULTRY FOR COOKING

All cooks should learn to cut up, bone, and pound poultry, even those who prefer to have the butcher perform this service for them. Whole and bone-in poultry is less expensive per pound and will allow the cook last-minute flexibility when deciding what to prepare.

CLEANING POULTRY

Before any preparation begins, all raw poultry, whether whole or cut up, should be washed and cleaned. Remove any bit of unappetizing fat, cartilage, or other matter that you wouldn't want to appear on the finished product.

Remove innards (neck and giblets) from cavity. Tear away any loose or large pieces of fat around both openings and from skin around neck. Insert hand into cavity and remove any tendons and fat that will pull away. Wash bird under cold running water inside cavity and out. Pat dry with paper towels.

BONING BREAST AND THIGHS FROM A WHOLE CHICKEN

Boneless thighs are elegant when served with a savory stuffing. Boned breasts are well suited to poaching, sautéing, and frying. To bone the breast and thighs from a whole chicken, first complete steps 1 through 4 for "Cutting Up a Whole Chicken" (see opposite page).

To bone breast: Remove legs from body. Insert boning knife flat against breastbone and run knife along bone to end of breast, releasing meat. Pull breast away from body; sever completely. Repeat with other breast half.

To bone thigh: With the fingers of one hand, grasp thigh meat parallel to thighbone. Using a boning knife, insert knife halfway into meat along one side of bone, beginning at one joint end. Run knife alongside bone, releasing meat on that side. Repeat on other side of bone to release that

meat; do not flip meat over. With boning knife, cut away any remaining meat from one joint end; lift thighbone and run boning knife underneath bone to completely sever. Sever at other joint end.

The rest of the chicken can be prepared as follows: *To remove wings:* Insert boning knife at joint and cut through to sever. If desired, remove wing tips by severing at joint with boning knife. Whole chicken is now in eight pieces: two boned half-breasts; two boned thighs; two drumsticks; two wings.

BONING A BREAST OFF THE BIRD

Poultry is sold in so many forms, cooks may need to bone a whole breast or breast halves already removed from the bird.

A whole breast is boned in the same way as the breast on a whole bird (see "Boning Breast and Thighs From a Whole Chicken," at left).

If you have two half-breasts, you will have one with the breastbone and ribs and one with just the ribs. To bone the half with the breastbone, insert boning knife along edge of breastbone where meat joins bone and release meat, cutting along the ribs if necessary. To bone the half without the breastbone, position breast with skin side up and narrow edge facing you and use boning knife to make a slit between bone and meat. Cut backwards along ribs to release meat.

POUNDING

For even cooking and an attractive appearance, boned meats should be pounded to a uniform thickness, usually about ¼ inch. To prevent meat from tearing, place it between two sheets of waxed paper. With the flat bottom of the meat pounder (not the edge that will shred the meat), pound with a downward stroke until the meat is evenly flattened.

CUTTING UP A WHOLE CHICKEN

Cutting up a whole fresh bird is in some ways similar to carving a cooked one (see page 112), except that here you are cutting through bone, which is not as easy to sever as a joint. You will need a boning knife, a heavy 8- or 10-inch chef's knife, and poultry shears. When done, you will have eight serving pieces: two breast halves; two thighs; two drumsticks; and two wings.

2. *After the joint has been exposed, separate leg from body by cutting through the skin to joint and severing leg at joint. Repeat for other leg.*

3. *Separate thigh and drumstick by cutting into leg at joint with boning knife; sever completely.*

1. *To expose the joint, hold on to the body with one hand and pull the leg away from the body with the other.*

4. *To remove whole breast from ribcage and wings, insert knife or poultry shears at the dividing line between breast and ribcage, beginning at wing joint. Cut along the edge of the ribcage, cutting through the cartilage between wing and breast. Repeat on other side; breast is now completely severed.*

5. *To halve breast, cut through the breastbone with a chef's knife.*

6. *Sever wing from back by cutting through at joint with chef's knife. Reserve back for stock.*

7. *When completed, cup-up chicken consists of two wings, two breast halves, two thighs, two drumsticks, plus the back.*

Plan a romantic dinner around Midnight Poussin (see page 24), a bird wrapped in pastry and roasted, just big enough to serve two in style.

Roasting & Baking

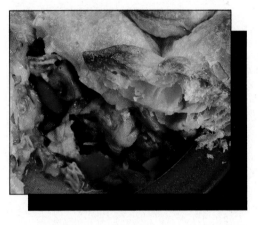

Roasting and baking are techniques for cooking food with currents of hot, dry air. Generally, the term roasting refers to the cooking of whole meats, while baking describes most other oven-cooked foods, such as cut-up poultry. In this chapter, you'll find a complete description of each technique, plus a raft of recipes utilizing each. Also included are step-by-step instructions for trussing poultry (see page 17), a selection of stuffing recipes (see pages 18-19), and a recipe for roasting the perfect turkey (see pages 22-23), as well as a menu that children can prepare (see pages 28-29).

ROASTING: COOKING WITH DRY HEAT

Probably no other dish is as familiar and as satisfying to American tastes as the roasted bird. A tender young fowl, seasoned to taste and its breast coated with butter, is set on a rack in a roasting pan. Perhaps a savory bread stuffing or a mix of coarsely chopped vegetables and fresh herbs is spooned into the bird's cavity before it goes into the oven. During cooking a wonderful transformation takes place. The bird plumps and its basted skin deepens to a nutty brown. Beneath its crisping surface, natural juices sealed in by the heat circulate through the meat fibers, adding flavor and moistness. Enticing aromas waft through the kitchen. Sounds of crackling fat and sizzling drippings call to the hungry and evoke images of other meals, and other places.

This simplest of cooking techniques is, however, also challenging to perfect. The French gastronome Brillat-Savarin said, "Cooks are made, roasters are born." Does that mean a perfectly roasted chicken comes only from the hands of a naturally gifted chef? Of course not! What he meant was that roasting is more than just timetables and thermometers. It requires both an understanding of the process and hands-on experience.

This chapter is intended to provide the understanding. As you cook, you will gain the experience.

WHAT IS ROASTING?

Roasting is one of the oldest and most widely used ways of preparing food. Lacking any utensils, our earliest ancestors roasted their food in hot ashes or on a stick over an open fire. During the Middle Ages, meat and fowl, spit-roasted in enormous open fireplaces, were popular banquet fare. It was not uncommon for each guest at an Elizabethan feast to be served a whole roasted bird and a large loaf of bread as one of many courses. The huge fireplaces of the Old World were duplicated in the kitchens of colonial America, complete with hand-turned spits and a recess in the fireplace wall for baking. Today we still roast by these methods, but more often we use a controlled-temperature oven.

The process of roasting involves currents of hot, dry air that cook raw food, making it suitable for us to eat. Roasting and its twin, baking, are the same process. Generally, roasting refers to the cooking of whole meats, including poultry, often with added fat. Most other oven-cooked foods—fish or bread or cut-up poultry, for instance—are thought of as being baked. On the other hand, ham is *baked* and chestnuts are *roasted*. These distinctions are more a matter of usage than an indicator of any real difference.

A Bird That's Fit to Eat

Heat plays a critical role in making poultry acceptable for human consumption. While beef and some fish can be eaten raw, poultry must reach a certain minimum internal temperature to be safe to eat. To avoid any risk of food poisoning, cooking times in poultry recipes are always long enough for the bird to reach the minimum safe internal temperature, no matter how inconsistent the oven or thermometer may be.

Health concerns aside, the bird would not be considered fit to eat by most of us when cooked only to the minimum internal temperature. Barely cooked, the muscle proteins would be soft and gelatinous. The color would be off and the juices tinged with red. Traditionally, Americans like their poultry well-done, with no transparency in the flesh or color in the juices. While the trend is toward cooking poultry less "done" than in the past, suggested temperatures even for medium-cooked poultry are still well above the safe minimum.

WHAT BIRDS TO ROAST?

A young, tender bird is the key to successful roasting. To test for tenderness, push against the bird's breastbone with your finger. The cartilage of a young fowl will give under this pressure.

The type of bird is up to you. Tiny *poussin* or Rock Cornish game hens are sized to serve one or possibly two. Larger broilers, fryers, roasting chickens, or meaty capons are other possibilities. In the fall, fresh-killed pheasant is available. Duck, quail, squab, and goose are sold all year, as is turkey. Most butchers will special-order any bird in season, given a few days' notice.

PREPARATION FOR ROASTING

Whatever you select—chicken, turkey, a game bird—the steps involved in readying the bird for the oven are basically the same.

Check to see that all the feathers have been removed. Usually they have been. If some remain, pluck them out with a pair of tweezers. Remove the innards and set them aside for gravy or stuffing, if desired. Wash the bird under running water and clean out the neck area and cavity. Remove lumps of fat that would be unpleasant to bite into when the bird is served. Be sure to pat the bird thoroughly dry; wet skin won't develop the sought-after brown color and crisp texture that are the hallmarks of well-roasted poultry.

(continued on page 18)

TRUSSING

Trussing is a method of securing the appendages of the bird close to the body. It holds the bird together during cooking, so that when finished, it has an attractive look. With stuffed poultry, trussing keeps the stuffing from falling out.

There are many ways to truss poultry. The simple tie method shown here is easy for the home cook to employ. If you wish, you can augment this method by closing up the cavity with small poultry skewers.

Some birds come with the legs held together by a metal clip, which serves the same purpose as trussing. All trussing, whether the metal clip or string, should be removed before the bird is served.

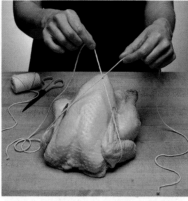

1. *Run a long piece of kitchen string under bottom of bird near neck end. Bring ends up and crisscross them over the breast, pinning the wings to the body.*

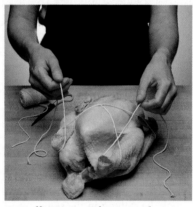

2. *Pull strings tight across breast and down around outside of bird. Wrap each string around a leg.*

3. *Complete loops around legs. Bring each string under tail and across to other side; pull to tighten, so legs and tail are drawn together.*

4. *Loop string around legs a second time.*

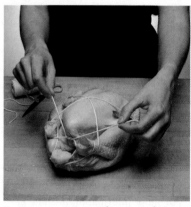

5. *Cross strings, tighten, and tie securely.*

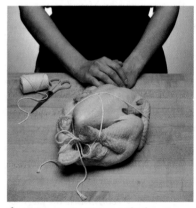

6. *Trim excess string. Chicken is now ready for cooking.*

ROAST TURKEY BREAST

Quick and easy to make for a week-night dinner, this is also great to have on hand for sandwiches for the family.

> 1 boneless turkey breast
>   (3 to 4 lbs)
>   Salt

1. Preheat oven to 400° F. Wash turkey breast and pat dry. Sprinkle with salt.

2. Place on a rack in a roasting pan. Set pan on middle rack of oven. Roast for 45 to 60 minutes, basting every 15 minutes after the first half hour.

3. When turkey breast is done, remove from oven and let rest for 10 minutes before slicing.

Serves 6 to 8.

MIDNIGHT POUSSIN

A wonderfully easy late-night dinner for two.

> ¼ cup chopped onion
>   Half a Granny Smith apple,
>   cored and cubed
> 1 piece crystallized ginger,
>   sliced, or 1 teaspoon ground
>   ginger
> 1 poussin (about 1 lb)
>   Salt
> 8½ ounces frozen puff pastry
>   (½ pkg), thawed
> 1 egg, lightly beaten

1. Preheat oven to 450° F. Grease a shallow baking dish slightly larger than the bird.

2. In a small bowl combine onion, apple, and ginger. Set aside.

3. Wash poussin and pat dry. Stuff with apple-onion mixture. Salt the outside of the poussin.

4. Roll out a piece of puff pastry to an 11- by 14-inch rectangle, ⅛ inch thick. Brush with beaten egg. Place pastry, coated side down, over the poussin. Fold around and under. Seal underneath by pinching together with fingers dipped in cold water. Brush top with beaten egg.

5. Place wrapped poussin in the baking dish. Set dish on middle rack of oven. Bake for 10 minutes. Cover crust loosely with an aluminum foil tent to prevent overbrowning. Bake 45 minutes more.

6. Remove from oven and allow to rest for 15 minutes.

Serves 2.

ROAST CHICKEN WITH GRAPES

A low-calorie version of a French classic, this dish uses Dijon mustard instead of the traditional white sauce.

> 1 frying chicken (about 3 lbs)
>   Salt
> 2 tablespoons Dijon mustard
> 1½ cups seedless green grapes
> ⅓ cup white wine
>   Dijon mustard

1. Preheat oven to 425° F. Remove innards and fat from chicken. Wash and pat dry; rub inside and out with salt and the 2 tablespoons mustard.

2. Fill chicken cavity with grapes; truss so the grapes stay put. Put on a rack in a roasting pan and set on middle rack of oven.

3. Roast for 40 minutes, basting several times with white wine and pan drippings.

4. After 40 minutes check doneness and, if desired, roast another 10 minutes.

5. Remove from oven and let rest for 20 minutes before carving.

6. Serve with grapes, pan drippings, and Dijon mustard.

Serves 4 to 6.

ROAST DUCK

In this recipe, the duck is turned from side to side instead of staying breast-up the whole time, so that the juices fall back into the meat rather than draining out, resulting in an especially tender duck. This method will work with any type of poultry. Chestnut Stuffing (see page 19) suits duck well. The stuffing can be baked in the bird or in a casserole.

> 1 duck (4½ to 5 lbs)
>   Salt

1. Preheat oven to 400° F. Remove giblets and excess fat from duck. Wash duck and pat dry. Prick the skin several times with the point of a knife to allow the fat to drain out during cooking. If duck is to be stuffed, do so at this point. Truss and salt thoroughly.

2. Place duck on one side on a rack in a roasting pan. Set pan on middle rack of oven.

3. Roast 20 minutes on one side (30 minutes if stuffed). Turn onto other side and roast 20 minutes (30 minutes if stuffed). Then turn breast side up and roast 20 minutes (30 minutes if stuffed). Each time you turn the duck, drain the fat that has accumulated in the roasting pan.

4. When duck is done to suit, remove from oven and allow it to rest 20 minutes before carving.

Serves 4.

ROASTED SMALL BIRDS

Small hens are charming for an intimate dinner. Complete the menu with wild rice, a sauce made from pan drippings, a vegetable mélange, and a good Beaujolais.

> 4 poussins or Rock Cornish
>   game hens (1 to 1½ lbs each)
>   Salt
> 8 slices uncooked bacon

1. Preheat oven to 450° F. Wash poussins or game hens and pat dry. Salt inside and out.

2. If birds are to be stuffed, do so at this point. Truss birds and lay two strips of bacon across each breast.

3. Set birds on a rack in a roasting pan and place pan on middle rack of oven. Roast for 30 minutes. Remove the bacon strips to allow the poultry to brown. Baste after removing bacon strips, and again when the birds are removed from the oven (15 more minutes if unstuffed, 30 more minutes if stuffed).

4. When poultry is done, let it rest 10 minutes before serving.

Serves 4.

MUSTARD MADNESS

This recipe is designed for a vertical roaster—an upright, stainless steel frame used to roast chicken and smaller birds. The vertical roaster cooks poultry faster than conventional methods because through the metal frame, an excellent heat conductor, the bird cooks from inside as well as outside, sealing in the natural juices.

    After cooking, large game hens can be halved to make four servings: With a sharp knife or poultry shears, begin to cut at the breastbone and continue along this line all the way around the bird.

> 2 Rock Cornish game hens (1
>   to 1½ lbs each)
>   Salt
>   Dijon mustard

1. Preheat oven to 450° F. Wash and dry game hens. Salt inside and out.

2. Set vertical roasters in a roasting pan containing ¼ inch of water. Lower game hens onto roasters. Truss wings to body of each bird. Paint each game hen with plenty of mustard.

3. Set pan on middle rack of oven and roast for 30 minutes.

4. When birds are done, remove them from oven and allow to rest for 30 minutes on frames. Remove from frames to serve.

5. Serve accompanied by additional Dijon mustard.

Serves 2 to 4.

Coated with spicy mustard, Rock Cornish game hens sit on stainless steel vertical roasters, ready for the oven. The frames conduct heat to the birds' interiors, producing a quickly cooked, succulent dish.

BAKING: THE SAME, YET DIFFERENT

Baking is one of the most versatile ways of preparing food, and poultry is no exception. Like roasting, baking is a method of cooking with dry heat. If you plan on baking a whole bird, choose a young and tender one. It's more common to bake cut-up poultry, sometimes in a wrap of foil, parchment, or pastry, in a porous clay pot, or topped with a sauce.

PARCHMENT AND FOIL

Enclosing poultry and selected flavorings in a sealed package of parchment paper or aluminum foil traps natural juices and steam-cooks the food, retaining a maximum of flavor and moisture. Cooking in parchment is best suited to delicate meats that are quickly done, such as fish or chicken breasts. This method is a boon to the calorie conscious, as no added fat or liquid is needed.

Parchment holds in heat and can keep a dish very warm for an extended period of time without overcooking. It is a wonderful no-fuss, no-mess way to entertain. Because few, if any, utensils are needed, there is little cleanup. The packages can be assembled early in the day, refrigerated, and brought to room temperature to bake. One of the delights of this technique is the wonderful fresh aroma that is released when the package is opened after cooking. When possible, open the parchment at the table as an extra treat for guests.

Parchment paper and aluminum foil are interchangeable, although parchment is more elegant. Whichever material you use, make sure to seal the package well so the juices don't leak out. For parchment, make a double fold and make little tears across the fold in several places to hold it shut.

CLAY POTS

Clay cooking pots have been excavated from Roman ruins dating back thousands of years. Like cooking in parchment, clay pot cookery allows poultry to bake in its own juices with little added fat. No basting is necessary. However, marinating the bird ahead of time will add a special flavor to the meat. Whole birds can be cooked with this technique and served with a sauce made from the liquid in the pot. Cooking in a clay pot is also like parchment cooking in that it produces little mess.

Do not preheat the oven when cooking with a clay pot. If exposed suddenly to high temperature, the pot will shatter. Before using, submerge the pot, top and bottom, in water for 15 minutes to seal the porous clay. This water is released as steam during cooking and keeps the bird moist. For easy cleanup, and to prevent the bird from sticking, line the pot with parchment paper.

BAKING IN PASTRY

Pastry doesn't always mean dessert. Always glamorous, pastry-wrapped foods are simple to prepare and should be in every cook's repertoire. Whole poultry, poultry pieces, and even ground poultry are all candidates for cooking with pastry, whether used as a total wrapping or as a flaky top crust.

To avoid soggy crusts—the number one problem—make sure that all cooked ingredients have been cooled, and that uncooked ingredients are as dry as possible. Keep sheets of filo dough between damp towels so they don't dry out and stiffen.

CHICKEN IN PROSCIUTTO

These succulent chicken rolls were inspired by a recipe from Giuliano Bugialli's wonderful book *Classic Techniques of Italian Cooking.*

> 2 *whole chicken breasts, boned, halved, and skinned*
> *Salt*
> 4 *thin slices prosciutto (see Note)*
> 4 *fresh basil leaves, for garnish*

1. Preheat oven to 350° F. Wash breast halves and pat dry. Salt breasts on both sides.

2. Halve prosciutto slices lengthwise. Lay 4 half-slices on a cutting board and cover each with a breast half; top each with second half-slice of prosciutto. Roll up and tie with kitchen string.

3. Place each roll on a 6- by 6-inch piece of aluminum foil. Seal and place foil packages on a baking sheet. Bake for 35 minutes.

4. Open packages, remove breasts, snip string, and garnish each breast with a basil leaf.

Serves 4.

Note If necessary, thin-sliced ham can be substituted for prosciutto.

CHICKEN 1-2-3

This tasty chicken dish was tested and approved as a fast weeknight dinner by a panel of working mothers.

> 2 *whole chicken breasts, boned, halved, and skinned*
> 4 *slices mozzarella cheese*
> 1 *jar (7 oz) marinara sauce*

1. Preheat oven to 350° F. Wash breast halves and pat dry; put into a 9-inch square baking pan. Top with mozzarella slices. Pour sauce over all. Cover with foil.

2. Bake for 30 minutes. Remove foil and bake an additional 10 minutes.

Serves 4.

CLAY POT PHEASANT WITH PIQUANT SAUCE

If at all possible, buy a fresh-killed pheasant. It makes a difference.

- 1 *pheasant (about 2 lbs)*
- ¼ *cup dry red wine*
- ¼ *cup red wine vinegar*
- 1 *clove garlic, crushed*
- 2 *tablespoons olive oil*
- 1 *tablespoon Worcestershire sauce*
- *Salt*
- 3 *tablespoons butter*
- 2 *to 3 green onions, julienned*

Piquant Sauce

- *Juices from baked pheasant*
- 1 *tablespoon cornstarch dissolved in 2 tablespoons water*
- 3 *tablespoons dry red wine*
- 1 *teaspoon red wine vinegar*
- 1 *teaspoon Dijon mustard*

1. *The day before:* Have butcher remove pheasant's neck or do it yourself at home. Wash pheasant and pat dry.

2. In a small bowl combine wine, vinegar, garlic, olive oil, and Worcestershire sauce.

3. Place pheasant in a nonporous dish and add marinade. Cover and refrigerate overnight. In the morning, turn pheasant over to marinate other side for 6 to 8 hours more.

4. *When ready to cook:* Immerse clay pot in water and soak for 15 minutes.

5. Drain pheasant, reserving marinade. Salt pheasant inside and out. Truss, and butter the breast liberally.

6. Line clay pot with parchment paper. Place pheasant in pot. Pour marinade over pheasant; scatter green onions on top. Cover with lid.

7. Set pot on center rack of a cold oven. Turn the oven to 475° F. Bake for 40 minutes. Remove lid and bake another 10 minutes to brown the skin. Remove pot from oven and set on a towel-covered surface so the hot pot won't crack from an extreme

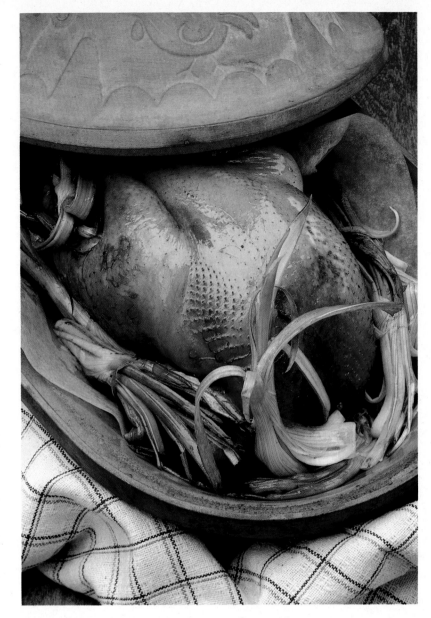

change in temperature. Remove pheasant from pot and let rest 15 minutes.

8. While bird is resting, prepare Piquant Sauce.

9. Carve pheasant and serve with Piquant Sauce.

Serves 3 to 4.

Piquant Sauce Skim fat from cooking liquids and pour remaining juices into a saucepan. Add cornstarch mixture and cook over medium heat until thickened. Add wine, vinegar, and mustard; whisk to blend. Just before serving, mix in the cooked green onion from the pheasant.

Clay Pot Pheasant is an elegant main course that makes few demands on the cook. As it bakes in the covered clay container, the bird bastes in its own juices, which become the base for a tangy sauce quickly made just before the dish is served.

menu

*This menu is easy
enough that kids can
prepare it. Perfect for
entertaining, the
turkey and
vegetables are
steamed in a
parchment package
that can be
assembled a day
ahead, refrigerated,
brought to room
temperature about
an hour and a half
before serving, and
then baked. For a
touch of drama,
open the package at
the table. Herbed
Butter should be a
staple in your freezer
to dress up broiled
meats and fish. The
recipe makes a
double batch; use
half for this dish and
freeze the remainder.*

PARCHMENT TURKEY WITH FRESH VEGETABLES

Melted butter
2 turkey fillets (about 1 to
1½ lbs total), skinned
2 yellow squash, sliced
2 zucchini, sliced in ½-inch
pieces
Half an onion, coarsely
chopped
One fourth of a red bell
pepper, sliced
Orange slices, for garnish

Herbed Butter

½ cup unsalted butter, softened
2 tablespoons chopped parsley
½ teaspoon salt
1 clove garlic, crushed
1 tablespoon snipped chives

1. Preheat oven to 400° F. Cut two 18-inch-long sheets of parchment paper; brush with melted butter. Place one piece, buttered side up, on a baking sheet.

2. Slice turkey fillets on the diagonal in ½-inch slices. Lay slices, long side facing you, in two parallel, overlapping rows down center of parchment.

3. Arrange yellow squash, zucchini, and onion around turkey. Dot turkey slices with ¼ cup of the Herbed Butter. Arrange red pepper slices on turkey.

4. Lay second parchment sheet, buttered side down, on top of turkey and vegetables. Fold edges under all the way around, sealing the packet. Bake 20 to 25 minutes. The parchment will puff.

5. Open parchment and serve turkey and vegetables immediately, garnished with orange slices.

Serves 4 to 6.

Herbed Butter In food processor or medium bowl of electric mixer, cream butter with parsley, salt, garlic, and chives. Shape in a block; chill 2 hours to set. Unused portion can be stored in freezer for up to 6 months.

Makes about ½ cup.

PARSLEYED RICE

2¼ cups water
1 teaspoon salt
1 cup rice, rinsed well
¼ cup chopped parsley
1 tablespoon butter

1. In a heavy saucepan bring water and salt to a boil. Add rice; reduce heat and simmer, covered, 20 minutes. Do not lift lid or stir.

2. After 20 minutes, fluff with a fork and stir in parsley and butter.

Serves 4 to 6.

ESPRESSO BROWNIES

4 squares (1 oz each)
unsweetened chocolate
½ cup unsalted butter
4 eggs
2 cups sugar
1 cup sifted flour
2 teaspoons instant espresso
coffee powder
1 tablespoon boiling water
1 teaspoon vanilla extract
1 package (6 oz) semisweet
chocolate chips
Vanilla ice cream

1. Preheat oven to 325° F. Grease a 9-inch square baking pan.

2. Melt chocolate and butter in a double boiler over hot water or in a bowl over a pan of hot water (a ceramic bowl will allow more control of the heat). Cool.

3. In a medium bowl beat eggs and sugar well. Blend in chocolate mixture, then flour.

4. Dissolve espresso powder in the water. Add to batter with vanilla.

5. Spread mixture in prepared pan and sprinkle chocolate chips over it.

6. Bake until a knife inserted in the center comes out clean (about 30 minutes). Cool and cut into 12 squares.

7. Serve with vanilla ice cream.

Makes 1 dozen brownies.

Parsleyed Rice and brownies are all that's needed to complete the meal when the main dish is turkey cooked in parchment with colorful vegetables.

The flaky pastry crust of Deep-Dish Chicken Pie contains a soul-satisfying filling of colorful vegetables and cubes of chicken, bound in a nutmeg-spiced sauce. Add a salad and dessert to make a meal.

DEEP-DISH CHICKEN PIE

Let this satisfying, homey American dinner pie warm a cold winter evening. To speed up preparation, cook the filling a day or two ahead and refrigerate it, covered. To serve, bring it to room temperature and proceed with step 4.

Pastry

1¼ cups flour
¼ teaspoon salt
¼ cup butter, cut in pieces
2 tablespoons lard, cut in pieces
1 egg
2 tablespoons cold water

Filling

¼ cup butter
1 small onion, chopped
¼ cup finely chopped celery
3 tablespoons flour
  Pinch each *freshly ground black pepper and freshly grated nutmeg*
2 cups chicken broth
6 cups cubed cooked chicken
½ cup fresh or frozen peas
¼ pound mushrooms, quartered
2 small carrots, peeled and sliced
  Salt and freshly ground black pepper

1. *To prepare pastry:* Sift flour and salt into a bowl. Cut butter and lard into flour with a pastry blender until mixture is crumbly.

2. Separate egg and reserve white. Beat yolk with the cold water and pour liquid into flour mixture. Stir with a wooden spoon until mixture begins to form a ball. With floured hands, lightly shape into a ball. Cover dough with waxed paper and refrigerate 1 hour.

3. *To prepare filling:* In a saucepan over medium heat, melt butter; add onion and celery and cook until soft. Stir in flour; cook until thickened. Add pepper and nutmeg. Gradually stir in broth, stirring constantly, until mixture bubbles and thickens. Mix in chicken, peas, mushrooms, and carrots. Season to taste. Set aside to cool.

4. *To assemble pie:* Preheat oven to 425° F. While filling cools, roll out the cold pastry on a floured surface into a 12-inch circle. Mix the reserved egg white with 1 tablespoon water; brush onto one side of pastry.

5. Pour cooled chicken mixture into a straight-sided, 9-inch-diameter baking dish about 2 inches deep. Place pastry, glazed side down, over filling. Trim pastry, flute edge, and cut slits in crust to allow steam to escape. Brush top with egg wash.

6. Bake until pastry is golden brown (30 to 40 minutes).

Serves 8.

CHICKEN AND MUSHROOM STRUDEL

Great served hot or cold, as a first course or as an entrée.

- 6 *tablespoons butter*
- 1 *medium onion, finely chopped*
- ½ *pound mushrooms, finely chopped*
- 1 *pound ground raw chicken*
- ½ *teaspoon salt*
- ½ *teaspoon dried tarragon*
- 1 *clove garlic, minced*
- ½ *cup freshly grated Parmesan cheese*
- ⅓ *cup diced prosciutto or ham*
- 1 *egg, beaten*
- 8 *sheets filo dough, thawed in refrigerator for 8 hours*

1. Preheat oven to 375° F. In a skillet melt 3 tablespoons of the butter; add onion and sauté over medium heat until golden. Add mushrooms and cook until soft. Add chicken, salt, tarragon, and garlic. Cook until chicken is browned. Mix in cheese, prosciutto, and egg.

2. *To assemble:* Place filo (between damp cloths so it does not dry out), remaining 3 tablespoons butter, melted, and a pastry brush near a cutting board or damp cloth.

3. Lay one sheet of filo on cutting board. Brush the half of sheet closest to you lightly but completely with butter. Spoon ⅓ cup of chicken mixture on narrow edge and fold in the sides. Roll up and place, seam side down, on a nonstick or lightly buttered baking sheet. Repeat with remaining sheets of dough.

4. Brush the rolls with remaining melted butter. Bake until golden brown (about 20 minutes).

5. For a first course, serve one roll per person; for an entrée serve two per person.

Makes 8 strudel rolls.

CHICKEN WELLINGTON WITH COGNAC CREAM SAUCE

The classic Beef Wellington stars a whole fillet of beef topped with foie gras and *duxelles,* then wrapped in puff pastry and baked. Sauce Périgueux is the crowning glory. In the following recipe, chicken breasts are teamed with chicken liver pâté and filo dough, then served with a wonderful Cognac-laced cream sauce to create a new twist on the famous classic. It is most important that the mushroom *duxelles* be squeezed as dry as possible to keep the crust from turning soggy. For the same reason, have all ingredients at room temperature.

- 3 *whole chicken breasts, boned, halved, skinned, and pounded until flat*
  Salt and freshly ground black pepper
- 12 *sheets filo dough, thawed in refrigerator for 8 hours*
- ⅓ *cup melted butter*
- 4 *tablespoons chicken liver pâté (see recipe on page 125, or use store-bought)*
- 2 *eggs, well beaten*

Duxelles

- 3 *pounds mushrooms, minced*
- 3 *to 4 tablespoons butter*
- 6 *shallots, finely chopped*
  Salt and freshly ground black pepper
  Cognac
- ⅓ *cup chopped parsley*

Cognac Cream Sauce

- 2 *tablespoons butter*
- 2 *tablespoons flour*
- 1½ *cups chicken broth*
- 2 *tablespoons Cognac*
- ¼ *cup whipping cream*

1. Preheat oven to 375° F. Wash chicken breasts and pat dry. Season with salt and pepper. Roll up and tie with kitchen string. Bake for 5 minutes on a baking sheet. Set aside to cool completely; remove string when cool.

2. Prepare Duxelles.

3. *To assemble:* Place filo dough (between damp cloths so it does not dry out), melted butter, and a pastry brush near a cutting board or damp cloth. Lay one sheet of filo on cutting board and brush lightly but completely with some of the melted butter. Place a second sheet of filo directly over the first. Place one half-breast on dough, toward one of the long sides. Spread about 2 teaspoons of the pâté on chicken and top with one sixth of the Duxelles.

4. Starting with the side the chicken is nearest, fold dough over half-breast. Fold opposite side over, around, and under chicken. Fold the other two sides under, trimming if there is too much dough. Seal seams with cold water. Repeat for rest of breast halves.

5. Place on a baking sheet, seam side down. Brush with egg. Bake until golden brown (20 to 25 minutes). Toward end of baking time, prepare Cognac Cream Sauce.

6. Serve each Wellington over Cognac Cream Sauce.

Serves 6.

Duxelles Wrap the minced mushrooms in a sheer towel or fine-mesh cheesecloth and squeeze out all excess moisture. In a skillet over medium heat, melt butter; add shallots and brown them. Add mushrooms, salt, and pepper and a few drops of Cognac. Stir over high heat until the moisture has evaporated. Stir in parsley. Cool completely.

Makes 1½ cups.

Cognac Cream Sauce In a saucepan melt butter; whisk in flour and cook until golden. Stir in broth and Cognac. Cook over medium heat until bubbles form and sauce thickens. Add cream, stirring constantly.

Makes 2 cups.

Grilling is a quick and flavorful method of cooking poultry. Here, Grilled Turkey Fillets With Cilantro and Salsa (see page 37) rest on a bed of rice.

Grilling & Broiling

The grill and the broiler cook with direct heat. The techniques are essentially the same; the distinction is that the grill imparts a unique smoky flavor. Poultry is ideal for direct-heat cooking: it cooks to tender doneness quickly, and its mildness means the flavor of the grilling process, or of marinades and sauces, can dominate the dish. In this chapter you'll find complete explanations of how to grill and broil to perfection, a menu for a backyard barbecue, California style (see pages 40-41), an elegant broiled duck dinner (see pages 48-49), and a collection of sauces and marinades (see pages 46-47).

COOKING WITH DIRECT HEAT

Today, the American Dream includes not only a chicken in every pot, as Herbert Hoover promised (and King Henry IV of France some three hundred years before him), but also one browning on the backyard barbecue as well.

Our country has an enduring infatuation with outdoor cooking, a romance that shows little sign of fading. Trend-setting restaurants have rushed to incorporate this ages-old technique into their repertoires. The diamond marking of the grill has become the hallmark of a new cuisine, and the grill chef has been elevated to culinary superstardom.

In turn, the creativity of food professionals has stimulated the home cook, who has long adhered to traditional barbecue methods and fare, to experiment with less-common fuels and new ingredients.

Cooking food over direct heat has taken on a sophistication unimagined in the days of the cowboy's simple campfire. But despite this big-city veneer, the appeal of barbecuing remains both elemental and immediate. We find warmth and comfort in the flame; we respond with gusto to the sight, sound, and smell of our food being cooked in front of us. Barbecuing is familiar, relaxing, and above all, makes food taste *wonderful*.

Poultry prepared on the grill or under the broiler (basically, oven grilling) has broad appeal, especially to a diet-conscious public demanding lighter meals with fewer sauces. Except for duck, poultry is naturally low in fat, and when properly cooked with dry heat, stays moist and tender. Its mild flavor won't overpower the subtle smoky essence the grilling process imparts. When broiled, it needs only simple seasoning to become an easily executed, always presentable last-minute meal. It welcomes all manner of marinades and sauces, is tender, and when cut in pieces, cooks quickly. The recipes in this chapter encompass such classics as tangy barbecued chicken and poultry-vegetable brochettes. You'll also find imaginative ideas in the *nouvelle* style, like turkey fillets with cilantro butter and a peppy tomato salsa, and smoked squab with apple-infused Calvados.

GRILLING AND BROILING: THE DIFFERENCE IS FLAVOR

Any poultry that can be grilled can be broiled—and vice versa. Both methods utilize dry, direct, *radiant* heat to achieve the same result—fowl cooked to a particular doneness with a characteristic browned surface. For this rapid, intense process, use only cut-up poultry, boned pieces, or the smallest whole birds. (Large whole birds will end up overdone on the outside and unappetizingly rare within.)

However, although grilling and broiling may be related methods, anyone who has tasted broiled poultry, and then a grilled version of the same dish, knows that their flavors are worlds apart. Broiling is a neutral heat source; it imparts no flavor of its own. Glowing charcoal, smoky wood briquettes, fragrant vine cuttings—all infuse grilled poultry with their essence. The resulting flavor is unique and cannot be duplicated with any other method, and it is why we cook over an open fire.

RADIANT HEAT

Radiant heat, which uses rays of energy to raise an object's temperature, is a boon—it is fast and promotes browning and flavor. However, a few minutes' inattention can suddenly change *browned* to *burned*. The frequent result—a charred surface with a half-done interior—is a major drawback of this method.

Broiled and grilled foods are cooked by both radiant energy and direct contact. Rays of heat warm the outer surface and then, by conduction, move through the food's interior mass. A delicate balance must be maintained between rapid surface cooking and slower, internal heat transfer. Control of the variables in this process—fuel, proximity to heat, thickness of the food, whether or not it has bones, and even the weather for those cooking outdoors—comes only with understanding of each cooking method and with practice.

ABOUT GRILLING

We probably discovered by accident that fire made our food taste better. One can imagine a piece of raw meat or dry grain falling into a fire and the discovery upon its retrieval that its appearance had changed—and so had its flavor. With time, humans learned that if the meat was held a short distance from the fire, it cooked more evenly and was more digestible.

Cooking over an open fire remained our primary method of food preparation for thousands of years. Not until this century was the technique relegated to the level of recreational activity and supplanted by more convenient and efficient gas- and electric-powered home appliances.

Open-fire cookery may appear simple, but to be successful, it requires constant attention. Starting the fire, maintaining an even temperature, achieving the correct distance from the heat, knowing when food is done, avoiding sudden flare-ups—all must be considered and understood.

EQUIPMENT

Basically, a *grill* is a cooking utensil with a grid of metal bars set over a heat source, which may be charcoal, wood, gas, or electricity. With proper equipment, grilling is possible indoors or out, at home or in a restaurant. The terms *grill* and *bar-*

becue are often used interchangeably. Barbecue has, perhaps, a more informal connotation, redolent of casual entertaining and down-home cooking. Purists and the U.S. Department of Agriculture, however, only consider foods cooked by direct heat over wood or charcoal real "barbecue."

Equipment is a matter of personal preference, available space, and frequency of use. Barbecue grills are sold as portable and built-in units, with and without lids, large enough to cook for a crowd, and sized for one or two persons. Real enthusiasts may be willing to commit money and kitchen space to a gas-fired or electric grill, which allows you to grill year-around. Like a broiler, these grills are convenient and easily regulated. However, they are also like a broiler in that they will not flavor food because they do not use vapor-emitting fuels.

FUEL

Backyard barbecuers commonly use charcoal briquettes. They are relatively easy to get going and are readily available. But some cooks, looking for a different flavor—and flavor is what open-fire cookery is all about—are experimenting with alternatives.

Lately much attention has been given so-called "new fuels" such as Mexican mesquite, fragrant fruit woods, oak and hickory chunks and chips—although none is really new. Just as some restaurants herald grilling as an innovation while others have been quietly preparing food this way for years, most of these "new" fuels have long histories in American cooking. Cooks in the Southwest, for instance, have used mesquite for more than a century.

Very young and tender birds (usually under six weeks of age and weighing about 1 pound), poussins make a nice alternative to serving chicken. Here, grilled poussin basted with lemon butter makes a savory main dish (see page 37).

A butterflied Rock Cornish game hen sizzles on the grill. To butterfly the small birds, cut along the backbone with poultry shears.

Wood chunks, chips, and cuttings are sought for their fragrance; they will not flavor the poultry unless the grill is quickly covered to trap the smoke (see "Smoking on the Grill"). Since the aroma of burning wood is pleasant for its own sake, try mixing a small amount of hickory, oak, manzanita, vine, or fruit tree (apple, cherry, fig) cuttings with charcoal for your grill. When gathering your own cuttings, take care that the trees have not been sprayed with pesticides. Both manzanita chips and grape vine cuttings are commercially marketed.

SMOKING ON THE GRILL

The dusky flavor of smoked poultry has many fans. To get a smoky flavor in your grilled poultry, soak wood chips or cuttings in a liquid for approximately two hours. You can use plain water or match the liquid to your recipe. For example, soak grape vines in wine, apple wood in apple juice, or manzanita in a liquor such as bourbon. Add the soaked chips to the fire during the last 15 minutes of grilling. Set the grill cover in place immediately or the smoke will dissipate and not be effective. You can also add other flavorings—orange and lemon rind, whole cloves, and nutmeg are recommended—at the same time you put the chips on the fire. Some herbs, particularly rosemary and bay leaves, will subtly flavor grilled poultry when added to the soaked chips. Again, use the grill cover to capture the herbal bouquet.

For basic grilling, charcoal—either briquettes or mesquite—is preferred. Wood burns too quickly and is better used for smoking, a technique that allows the wood's fragrance to enter the food.

Many chefs prefer mesquite charcoal, made from a Mexican hardwood. It burns very hot, perhaps twice as hot as briquettes, and therefore cooks food faster, searing in juices. It imparts a subtle, natural flavor. Mesquite coals can be used two or even three times before they need to be replaced. On the negative side, mesquite can be difficult to start and expensive. Although it is not as easy to find as briquettes, well-stocked cookware shops, hardware stores, upscale supermarkets, specialty stores, and mail-order catalogs do carry it. Some wholesalers will also sell it retail by mail.

GRILLED ROCK CORNISH GAME HENS

Small game birds work well either grilled or broiled. In this recipe, the game hens are butterflied for ease of handling and quick cooking.

> 2 tablespoons butter, softened
> 2 tablespoons minced shallots
> 2 Rock Cornish game hens
>   (1 lb each)
>   Salt

1. In a small bowl combine butter and shallots until well blended. Set aside.

2. Cut along backbone of game hens with poultry shears. Open up birds to create a butterfly effect. Lightly salt both sides.

3. Prepare fire. When coals are ready, place game hens, breast side down, on grill; sear. Turn; sear other side.

4. Grill game hens, brushing frequently with the shallot butter, until the flesh springs back slightly when touched (about 10 to 12 minutes).

Serves 2.

GRILLED TURKEY FILLETS WITH CILANTRO AND SALSA

The flavors found in Mexican cuisine appeal to many chefs today. Here cilantro, also called Chinese parsley, seasons a compound butter brushed on the turkey as it grills. The salsa recipe comes from Arizona and must be prepared a day ahead so the flavors will blend.

> *¼ cup butter, softened*
> *½ cup minced cilantro leaves*
> *4 turkey fillets, halved lengthwise*

Judith's Salsa

> *8 fresh tomatoes, peeled and seeded*
> *1 can (4 oz) green chiles, chopped*
> *¼ cup minced cilantro leaves*
> *3 green onions, chopped*
> *2 tablespoons dried oregano*
> *1 clove garlic, minced*
> *¼ cup lemon juice*
> *1 can (4 oz) jalapeño peppers, minced*

1. A day in advance, prepare the salsa.

2. In a small bowl combine softened butter with cilantro. Set aside. Wash turkey fillets and pat dry.

3. Prepare fire. When coals are ready, lay turkey fillets diagonally across grill bars. When fillets are seared, lift them and set back on grill along opposite diagonal. When diamond pattern appears on the surface, turn fillets over and sear diamond pattern onto other side.

4. Grill 5 inches from heat, brushing both sides of fillet with cilantro butter, about 8 minutes.

5. Serve dotted with remaining cilantro butter and Judith's Salsa.

Serves 6 to 8.

Judith's Salsa In a food processor or blender, purée all ingredients *except* jalapeño peppers until smooth. Mix in peppers, 1 tablespoon at a time, to taste. Let salsa sit overnight in the refrigerator to marry flavors.

Makes 4 cups.

POUSSIN WITH LEMON BUTTER

The smoky-sweet flavor of grilled poussin delights the senses. The accompanying compound butter adds a refreshing snap of citrus to these delectable birds.

> *½ cup butter, softened*
> *2 tablespoons lemon juice*
> *Grated rind of 1 lemon*
> *2 poussins (1 lb each)*
> *1 small bunch fresh marjoram*
> *Salt*

1. In a bowl combine butter, lemon juice, and lemon rind. Set aside.

2. Wash poussins and pat dry. Stuff each with marjoram. Tie legs together with kitchen string, and tuck wings under. Lightly salt outsides.

3. Prepare fire. When coals are ready, place poussin on grill, breast side down. Sear breasts. Turn and sear back. Turn on each side and sear.

4. Grill 5 inches from heat, brushing frequently with lemon butter, until poussin springs back slightly when touched (about 25 minutes).

5. To serve, snip kitchen string. Remove marjoram and serve as a garnish. Melt remaining lemon butter and pass as dipping sauce.

Serves 2 to 4.

... FOR GRILLING POULTRY

☐ *Allow 30 minutes—longer on a cool or windy day—for charcoal briquettes to heat to the gray-ash stage. Mesquite charcoal may require 45 minutes. Coals are hot enough when you can hold your hand over the grill for no more than 3 seconds. Clean the grill rack thoroughly before cooking, then brush it with oil and adjust it so that food will be 5 to 6 inches from the heat.*

☐ *Poultry should be at room temperature, about 70° F. Trim off excess fat.*

☐ *To keep the poultry meat moist and juicy, quickly sear it on both sides, then proceed with the grilling. To obtain the distinctive diamond grill mark, set the poultry on a hot grill diagonally to the bars, then lift it and set it back on the grill on the opposite diagonal.*

☐ *Have ready a spray bottle filled with water to douse flare-ups. Use long, wood-handled utensils— tongs, a spatula, and a basting brush—and an asbestos mitt.*

☐ *Poultry is done when a meat thermometer inserted in the thickest part reads 170° F to 175° F, or when the juices run just slightly pink when the skin is pierced. The flesh should spring back slightly when touched. Approximate grilling times: cut-up pieces of chicken or turkey with bone, 50 to 70 minutes; small whole birds, 25 minutes; halved game hens, 12 to 20 minutes, depending on weight; brochettes, 10 to 15 minutes; boned breasts, 5 to 10 minutes.*

SMOKED, STUFFED SQUABS WITH CALVADOS

Smoking the squabs is easy. Soak apple cuttings in water mixed with apple juice for two to four hours. When the fire is hot, put the cuttings atop the coals, place the squabs on the grill, and set the cover in place. The resulting smoke will flavor the squabs with the essence of apple.

- *⅓ cup apple juice*
- *⅓ cup Calvados (see Note)*
- *⅓ cup vegetable oil*
- *2 squabs (about ¾ lb each)*

Stuffing

- *¼ cup Calvados (see Note)*
- *Half a pippin apple, cubed*
- *1 shallot, minced*

Calvados Sauce

- *½ cup apple juice*
- *¼ cup Calvados*
- *1 tablespoon cornstarch mixed with 2 tablespoons water*

1. Make Stuffing. Set aside.

2. In a medium bowl combine apple juice, Calvados, and vegetable oil to make marinade.

3. Wash squabs and pat dry. Set in a pan just big enough to hold both birds. Pour marinade over squabs and marinate in refrigerator for 4 hours.

4. Remove squabs from marinade, reserving marinade for basting, and pat squab dry.

5. Insert Stuffing into squabs and tie legs together with kitchen string; tuck wings under.

6. Prepare fire. When coals are ready, grill squabs 5 inches from heat, breast side down, with the cover on the grill so that the smoke can penetrate the meat.

7. After 15 minutes turn squabs breast side up. Continue grilling, basting frequently with marinade, until breast meat springs back slightly when touched (about 10 minutes).

8. To serve, snip kitchen string and remove. Spoon out Stuffing and serve on the side. Smother squabs with Calvados Sauce.

Serves 2.

Note If necessary, applejack can be substituted for the Calvados.

Stuffing In a small bowl combine Calvados, apple, and shallot.

Calvados Sauce In a small saucepan combine apple juice, Calvados, and cornstarch paste. Simmer until thickened.

Makes ¾ cup.

BARBECUED CHICKEN WITH TWO SAUCES

Real, red-bandana, down-home barbecued chicken has been an American favorite since pioneer days. To satisfy all tastes, you have a choice of two sauces—one, sweet and tangy, the other with a little more punch.

To get more sauce on the chicken, you might want to try this alternate cooking method: After the chicken pieces have been on the grill for about 40 minutes, remove them to a platter and set aside. Cut a piece of heavy-duty aluminum foil about 2 inches larger than the perimeter of the grill surface and roll up the edges to form a rim. Lay the foil on the grill. With a carving fork or skewer, poke 8 to 10 holes in the foil, spaced at regular intervals. Set the chicken on the foil-covered grill and generously coat with barbecue sauce. Grill another 20 minutes. The chicken will not be as brown as if cooked directly on the rack, but it will be more thoroughly coated with sauce.

- *1 chicken (3 to 4 lbs), cut up*
- *1 cup barbecue sauce*

Sweet and Mild Barbecue Sauce

- *2 tablespoons butter*
- *Half a large red onion, minced*
- *½ cup catsup*
- *½ cup water*
- *2 tablespoons apple cider vinegar*
- *1 tablespoon brown sugar*
- *A few drops hot-pepper sauce*

Hot and Spicy Barbecue Sauce

- *½ cup catsup*
- *½ cup white wine*
- *2 teaspoons Worcestershire sauce*
- *2 cloves garlic, crushed*
- *½ teaspoon chili powder*
- *A few drops hot-pepper sauce*

1. Remove any excess fat from chicken pieces, wash chicken, and pat dry.

2. Prepare fire. When coals are ready, place chicken on grill, skin side down. When seared, turn skin side up.

3. After about 30 to 40 minutes, baste chicken with sauce, turning pieces frequently to prevent charring. Grill until the chicken springs back slightly when touched (about 50 to 60 minutes).

Serves 4.

Sweet and Mild Barbecue Sauce
In a medium saucepan over moderate heat, melt butter and sauté onion. Add catsup, water, vinegar, brown sugar, and hot-pepper sauce. Stir until blended. Increase heat and bring sauce to a boil. Reduce heat and simmer 15 to 20 minutes. Cool.

Makes 1 cup.

Hot and Spicy Barbecue Sauce
In a medium saucepan combine catsup, wine, Worcestershire sauce, garlic, chili powder, and hot-pepper sauce. Bring to a boil. Reduce heat and simmer 20 minutes. Cool.

Makes 1 cup.

For the barbecue fan, grilled chicken with a choice: a mild sauce sweetened with brown sugar or a spicy one with the heat of chili powder.

menu

CALIFORNIA BARBECUE

Chicken and Seafood Grill

Vegetable Mélange With Almond Vinaigrette

Fusilli Salad

French Bread With Herbed Goat Cheese

Frozen Strawberry Torte

Sparkling Cassis

Imagine a warm summer day. The cheese is marinating, the pasta is cooking, and the grill is hot—all is ready for a barbecue, California style.

The Vegetable Mélange was inspired by the New York catering firm of Glorious Food. The vegetables can be blanched ahead, tossed with the vinaigrette, then refrigerated. The frozen torte must be prepared the day before as it needs 12 hours in the freezer to set.

CHICKEN AND SEAFOOD GRILL

- 2 whole chicken breasts, halved, boned, and skinned
- 8 scallops
- 8 jumbo shrimp, peeled and deveined
- 4 thin slices prosciutto
  Vegetable oil, for basting

1. Slice boned breast halves lengthwise into three or four ½-inch slices. Wash sliced chicken and pat dry.

2. Wash and pat dry scallops and shrimp. Halve each prosciutto slice lengthwise.

3. *To assemble:* On an 8-inch skewer alternately thread prosciutto, chicken, and seafood, weaving the slice of prosciutto around and under the fish and poultry. Repeat with seven more skewers.

4. Grill or broil 5 inches from heat, brushing with oil and turning occasionally, about 10 minutes.

Makes 8 brochettes.

VEGETABLE MÉLANGE WITH ALMOND VINAIGRETTE

- 1 carrot, peeled, julienned, and blanched
- 1 zucchini, julienned and blanched
- ½ pound snow peas, trimmed and blanched
- ½ pound green beans, julienned and blanched

Almond Vinaigrette

- ⅔ cup almond oil
- ⅓ cup tarragon vinegar
- 1 teaspoon dried tarragon
  Pinch each of salt, sugar, and freshly ground black pepper

In a medium bowl toss vegetables together and set aside. Prepare Almond Vinaigrette and pour over vegetables; toss. Serve lukewarm or cold.

Serves 4.

Almond Vinaigrette In a small bowl whisk together oil, vinegar, tarragon, salt, sugar, and pepper.

Makes 1 cup.

FUSILLI SALAD

- 8 cups water
- 1 tablespoon salt
- 8 ounces dry fusilli
- 2 tablespoons olive oil
- 1 teaspoon white wine vinegar
- 2 teaspoons chopped fresh basil
- 1 clove garlic, minced
- ½ cup whipping cream
- 1 egg yolk
  Salt and freshly ground black pepper
- ½ cup raw peas
- ½ cup cubed yellow squash
- ½ cup cubed tomato

1. In a large pot over medium-high heat, bring the water and salt to a boil. Add pasta, stir well, and cover. Return to a boil and cook pasta until just tender.

2. Drain pasta in a colander and transfer to a large bowl. Toss with 1 tablespoon of the olive oil, the vinegar, and basil. Set aside to cool.

3. In a medium saucepan sauté garlic in remaining tablespoon olive oil. Pour in whipping cream and heat to just below boiling. Turn off heat.

4. In a small bowl mix a little of the hot cream with egg yolk. Pour mixture back into cream sauce; blend well to thicken sauce. Season with salt and pepper and set aside to cool.

5. In a medium skillet with a small amount of water, lightly steam peas and yellow squash. When they are tender-crisp, toss with tomato and pasta. Pour sauce over all, toss again, and serve at room temperature.

Serves 4.

HERBED GOAT CHEESE

- 2 rounds (4 oz each) soft chèvre
- ⅓ cup olive oil
  Fresh or dried rosemary
  French bread for accompaniment

1. Arrange goat cheese on a small platter.

2. Pour oil over cheese and sprinkle with fresh or dried rosemary.

3. Serve with slices of fresh French bread.

Serves 4.

FROZEN STRAWBERRY TORTE

Crust

- 1 cup graham cracker crumbs
- 3 tablespoons sugar
- ½ cup chopped pecans
- ¼ cup butter, melted

Filling

- 4 cups sliced strawberries (about 3 pts)
- 1 cup sugar
- 2 egg whites
- 1 tablespoon lemon juice
- 1 teaspoon vanilla extract
- ⅛ teaspoon salt
- ½ cup whipping cream

1. *To prepare crust:* Preheat oven to 325° F. In medium bowl mix crumbs, sugar, pecans, and butter. Press into bottom of 10-inch springform pan. Bake 10 minutes; cool completely.

2. *To prepare filling:* In a large bowl combine 2 cups of the sliced strawberries with sugar, egg whites, lemon juice, vanilla, and salt. With an electric mixer beat on low speed to blend, then on high speed until firm peaks form (about 15 minutes).

3. In a medium bowl beat whipping cream with an electric mixer until soft peaks form.

4. *To assemble torte:* Gently fold whipped cream into berry mixture. Pour into cooled crust. Cover; freeze until very firm (about 12 hours).

5. When ready to serve, purée remaining 2 cups strawberries. Pour some purée over each slice of torte.

Serves 8.

Brochettes of chicken, scallops, and shrimp are the focus of a casual yet elegant outdoor meal that also includes herbed cheese with French bread, julienned vegetables, pasta salad, and frozen fresh-strawberry torte for dessert.

Chicken-wing drummettes, perfectly sized for finger foods, broil quickly to make these tempting Sesame Appetizers.

ABOUT BROILING

Oven broiling is essentially indoor grilling using electric or gas heat. As with grilling, broiling heats food one side at a time. It is appreciated for its convenience, speed, and simplicity. With the cooking device built into the oven, there are no grills to transport, no added fuel, no coals to dispose of afterwards. It is quick to start; pre-heating is accomplished in one third of the time it takes to ready coals.

Broiled poultry is a staple in the diets of those seeking to restrict their intake of fats. Tender, young poultry has little natural fat, and broiling allows what fat there is to drain into the broiler pan. However, a certain amount of fat—a marinade or a baste—must be applied to the poultry to keep the flesh from drying out. Marinades and bastes are also wonderful for adding flavor to broiled poultry. Be sure, though, to drain oil-based sauces from the meat before cooking, to prevent fires.

As is the case with grilling, only small, tender cuts of poultry respond to the fast, radiant heat of broiling. Cut-up poultry pieces have less mass to heat than large whole birds, which means the inside will cook to done-ness in the same amount of time it takes the outside to brown. Turkey and chicken parts and fillets, as well as cut-up game hens, poussins, and pheasant, are appropriate for broiling.

Broiled items should be uniform in size. Broiled and grilled poultry always tastes better cooked to a medi-um, rather than well-done, stage. To determine doneness in larger pieces, use an instant-read meat ther-mometer inserted in the thickest part of the flesh. Poultry is ready at 170° F to 175° F; at this stage, juices will run just slightly pink. With small poultry pieces using a thermometer is not practical. Instead, press the flesh with your finger or tongs. When cooked, the meat will spring back slightly.

With experience, the home cook will get a sense of the balance of time and distance from heat needed to broil a particular type and size of poultry to juicy doneness. Because the rays of radiant heat spread out and are less concentrated as they travel from their source, the farther a piece of poultry is from the heat source, the more time it can stay under the broiler before overcooking. Thus larger pieces of poultry, requiring a longer broiling time than thin fillets or skewered foods, may need to be set on a low oven rack to ensure a nicely browned surface and properly cooked interior. Experiment with your broil-er's temperature controls and rack settings. As you cook, you will get to know the limits of your particular equipment.

SESAME APPETIZERS

Sesame seeds get a rich nutty taste when toasted. Toast your own in a heavy-bottomed skillet over high heat, shaking the pan, until the seeds are golden brown and a pungent sesame aroma fills the air (about 5 minutes). Chicken drummettes are not drumsticks but part of the chicken wing. They come in packages and make wonderful hors d'oeuvres.

- ½ cup vegetable oil
- ½ cup sherry
- 4 tablespoons soy sauce
- 4 tablespoons lemon juice
- 2 cloves garlic, minced
- 4 tablespoons toasted sesame seed
- 2 pounds chicken drummettes
  Salt

1. In a blender combine oil, sherry, soy sauce, lemon juice, garlic, and sesame seed. Process until smooth.

2. Wash drummettes and pat dry. Salt lightly. Place in a large bowl and cover with sherry marinade. Refrigerate for at least 1 hour.

3. Preheat broiler. Broil drummettes 5 inches from heat for 7 minutes per side, basting once on each side with marinade.

Makes about 20 drummettes.

PLUM PHEASANT

A damson plum sauce complements any poultry dish. Here it enhances the mild flavor of pheasant with a lively sweet-and-sour taste.

- ½ cup damson plum jelly
- 1 tablespoon catsup
- 1 tablespoon apple cider vinegar
- ¼ teaspoon dry mustard
- 2 tablespoons soy sauce
- 4 pheasant legs

1. In a small bowl mix jelly, catsup, vinegar, mustard, and soy sauce.

2. Wash pheasant legs and pat dry.

3. Preheat broiler. Place pheasant legs on broiler pan and brush with plum sauce.

4. Broil 5 inches from heat for about 5 minutes. Turn, baste with sauce, and broil 5 minutes more.

5. Serve with remaining plum sauce.

Serves 2 to 4.

GINGERED GAME HEN

For a quick but charming dinner for two, serve this bird with rice pilaf, sautéed apples, and a three-lettuce salad tossed with a raspberry vinaigrette.

- 1 Rock Cornish game hen (about 1½ lbs)
  Slice of fresh ginger

Ginger-Wine Sauce

- ¼ cup olive oil
- 2 tablespoons dry red wine
- ½ teaspoon honey
- 2 tablespoons minced red onion
- 1 clove garlic, minced
- ½ teaspoon grated fresh ginger

1. Clean, wash, and dry game hen. With poultry shears, halve bird, starting at backbone and continuing along breastbone. Rub skin with slice of fresh ginger.

2. Prepare Ginger-Wine Sauce. Brush both sides of each game-hen half with sauce.

3. Preheat broiler. Set game-hen halves, skin side down, on broiler pan.

4. Broil 5 inches from heat, 8 to 10 minutes per side. Brush every 3 to 4 minutes with sauce.

Serves 2.

Ginger-Wine Sauce In a blender combine olive oil, wine, honey, onion, garlic, and ginger and process until smooth.

... FOR BROILING POULTRY

- ☐ *Always preheat your broiler. If it's electric, leave the door ajar when the unit is in operation.*

- ☐ *Line the inside of the broiling pan with aluminum foil to ease cleanup.*

- ☐ *Do not preheat the pan; the poultry will sear and adhere to the hot surface. Oiling the pan prevents sticking.*

- ☐ *Trim excess fat from poultry before broiling since fat can ignite from high heat. For the same reason, drain off oil-based marinades and pat meat dry.*

- ☐ *Split or halve small birds to promote even broiling.*

- ☐ *Start poultry skin side down to prevent too-rapid browning and to reduce shrinkage.*

- ☐ *Broil 3 to 5 inches from heat, depending on the thickness of the food. Five inches is the recommended distance for most recipes.*

- ☐ *Broiled foods are done when a meat thermometer inserted in the thickest part of the flesh reads 170° F to 175° F, or when the juices run slightly pink, or when the flesh springs back slightly when touched. Approximate broiling times: cut-up pieces of chicken or turkey with bone, 50 to 70 minutes; small whole birds, 25 minutes; halved game hens, 12 to 20 minutes, depending on weight; brochettes, 10 to 15 minutes; boned breasts, 5 to 10 minutes.*

Chicken Brochettes With Garden Vegetables—sliced chicken breasts with red pepper, red onion, mushrooms, zucchini, and yellow squash—make a colorful company meal that's easy on the cook.

BROCHETTES: FESTIVE, FUN, FAST

Pieces of boned poultry, colorful vegetables, spicy meat, subtle seafood arranged on a skewer—*brochettes* are especially suited for grilling and broiling. Skewered foods can be casual or formal. Boneless and trimmed of any indigestible fat, they are completely edible. Whether served as an appetizer or as an entrée, brochettes are simple, attractive, and always popular with guests.

The recipes that follow require only quick cooking and can be assembled well ahead of time. It's easy to gauge portions as well: As a rule, two brochettes make one main course serving.

SESAME CHICKEN WITH SNOW PEAS

For extra flavor baste the chicken with Japanese Sauce (see page 47), and serve the remainder of the sauce with the brochettes.

    4 whole chicken breasts, boned,
       halved, and skinned
 1½ pounds snow peas, washed
       and trimmed
    ½ cup sesame oil

1. Prepare fire or preheat broiler. Wash boned chicken breast halves and pat dry. Cut each breast half into 3 slices.

2. *To assemble:* Alternate 1 piece of chicken with 3 snow peas on 8-inch skewers, until skewers are filled.

3. Grill or broil 5 inches from heat for about 8 minutes per side, brushing frequently with sesame oil.

Makes 8 brochettes.

MIDDLE EASTERN TURKEY KABOBS

To create a Middle Eastern mood, serve these brochettes as a light luncheon, with couscous, marinated tomatoes and cucumbers, Lebanese date cookies, and mint tea. Japanese eggplants are small, about 6 inches long and 2 inches wide, and are generally available at better produce markets.

    4   cups yogurt
    1   cup minced parsley
    8   cloves garlic, minced
    1   teaspoon cumin
    4   turkey fillets, cut in
        1- by 1-inch squares
    4   Japanese eggplants, cut in
        1-inch rounds and parboiled

1. In a medium bowl combine yogurt, parsley, garlic, and cumin.

2. Marinate turkey in the yogurt mixture for 4 hours, covered, in the refrigerator. Remove turkey from marinade, set marinade aside, and pat turkey dry.

3. Prepare fire or preheat broiler. *To assemble:* Alternate turkey pieces with eggplant rounds on 8-inch skewers.

4. Grill or broil 5 inches from heat about 8 minutes per side, basting frequently with yogurt marinade.

Makes 8 brochettes.

SKEWERED CHICKEN LIVERS

After a taste of this wonderful appetizer, even people who don't like liver will ask for more.

    2   bunches green onions
    1   pound chicken livers,
        washed and dried

1. Prepare fire or preheat broiler. Wash green onions and remove roots. Trim the greens so that 4 inches remain.

2. *To assemble:* Alternate livers and green onions on 8-inch skewers.

3. Grill or broil 5 inches from heat about 5 minutes per side.

Makes 4 brochettes.

CHICKEN BROCHETTES WITH GARDEN VEGETABLES

Colorful, flavorful, and fresh, these chicken brochettes are a cinch to prepare. A mustard-and-wine marinade, seasoned with herbs, adds extra flavor.

    2   whole chicken breasts, boned,
        halved, and skinned
        Salt
        Half a red pepper, cut in
        1-inch squares
        One fourth of a red onion,
        cut in 1-inch squares
    8   mushroom caps, wiped clean
    1   zucchini, cut into ½-inch slices
    1   yellow squash, cut into
        ½-inch slices

White Wine Marinade

    ¼   cup vegetable oil
    ½   cup dry white wine
    1   teaspoon Dijon mustard
    1   tablespoon minced parsley
    ⅛   teaspoon dried thyme
    ⅛   teaspoon salt
        Pinch paprika

1. Slice chicken breast halves into 1- by 2-inch strips; salt lightly and set aside.

2. Prepare White Wine Marinade. In a large bowl combine chicken strips and marinade and refrigerate, covered, for 2 hours. Drain chicken, reserving marinade; pat chicken dry.

3. Prepare fire or preheat broiler. *To assemble:* Alternate chicken and vegetables on 8-inch skewers. Brush with remaining marinade.

4. Grill or broil 5 inches from heat for 7 minutes per side, brushing with marinade on each side.

Makes 8 brochettes.

White Wine Marinade In a blender combine oil, wine, mustard, parsley, thyme, salt, and paprika.

Makes about ¾ cup.

TIPS FOR PREPARING SKEWERS

☐ *On a single skewer, combine foods that will cook in the same amount of time, or blanch slower-cooking elements ahead of time.*

☐ *Skewers can be metal or wood. They should be flat-sided if possible so the ingredients don't slip around when the skewer is rotated.*

☐ *When you use bamboo skewers, presoak them for an hour to keep them from burning when exposed to high heat.*

☐ *If all ingredients on a brochette require a relatively long cooking time, consider precooking them, then grilling or broiling as the final step to add color.*

☐ *Either grilled or broiled, skewered foods usually cook in 6 to 12 minutes.*

PHEASANT BROCHETTES WITH BABY VEGETABLES

Baby vegetables, available at specialty markets and better produce sections of supermarkets, are especially charming *en brochette*. They must be slightly precooked to match the cooking time of the pheasant. If desired, chicken or turkey can be substituted for the pheasant.

    2 whole pheasants (about 2½ lbs each)
   12 baby carrots, peeled and blanched
    4 baby artichokes, trimmed and parboiled

Tarragon-Mustard Sauce

   ¼ cup Dijon mustard
   ¼ cup tarragon vinegar
   ¼ cup vegetable oil

1. Have butcher remove pheasants' necks (or do it yourself at home). Wash pheasants and pat dry. Remove breast meat from carcass; reserve carcass for stock. Legs can be used for Plum Pheasant (see page 43).

2. Prepare fire or preheat broiler. Slice each breast in half lengthwise and then into 6 equal pieces each.

3. *To assemble:* Alternate pheasant strips with carrots on 8-inch skewers, ending each skewer with a whole baby artichoke.

4. Prepare Tarragon-Mustard Sauce. Grill or broil brochettes 5 inches from heat about 6 to 8 minutes per side, basting frequently with sauce.

5. Serve the brochettes with remaining sauce.

Makes 4 brochettes.

Tarragon-Mustard Sauce In a small bowl combine mustard, vinegar, and oil; whisk vigorously to blend.

MARINADES AND BASTING SAUCES

The addition of a marinade or a baste enhances the flavor of grilled or broiled poultry. Typically, these sauces are made of oil, seasoning, and an acid such as lemon juice or vinegar. The acid breaks down muscle fiber for a more tender final product, while the oil adds to our appreciation of the food: studies have shown that foods containing fat have a better "mouth feel."

Marinades and bastes are almost identical, differing mainly in their application. However, a basting sauce often contains more oil than a marinade to help the sauce stick to the meat. Basting sauces simply impart surface flavor and help keep foods moist; they do not tenderize. Marinades, on the other hand, do tenderize, because the time elapsed during marination allows the acid to act upon the muscle fiber.

Foods usually sit in marinades for at least an hour or as long as overnight, depending on the quantity of poultry and the amount of preparation time available to the cook. Cubed poultry and small portions generally marinate for two to three hours. Larger cuts are best marinated overnight. If you are marinating longer than an hour, put the poultry in the refrigerator to eliminate the chance that harmful bacteria will develop. Remove the poultry from the refrigerator about 30 minutes before cooking to bring it closer to room temperature—since cold poultry will take longer to cook.

Fat may cause a flare-up on the grill or in the broiler, so before cooking, drain the marinade from the poultry and pat it dry. Also, the sugars in both marinades and bastes lower the browning temperature. Cooks must be vigilant to see that the caramelizing sugars brown and do not burn.

Basting sauces are added during cooking. Don't baste as soon as the poultry is set on the grill or in the broiler, or the meat may burn and its skin get too crisp and dry. Baste about two thirds of the way through the cooking time, or during the last 15 minutes.

In addition to their use in preparation, most marinades and bastes are also good served on the side as a dipping sauce for the cooked poultry.

How Much Sauce to Make?

Allow about ⅓ cup of sauce per pound of poultry. If you have a blender, use it to mix the sauce rather than doing it by hand. The blender's rapid action is ideal for emulsifying and dispersing the ingredients in the liquid. A food processor works equally well, but its container is oversized for the amount of sauce usually made. Always use a noncorrosive container, such as glass or stainless steel, to prepare acid-based sauces. Otherwise the sauce will eat away the container's surface and spoil both container and marinade.

VERSATILE MARINADES AND BASTES

Each of the following recipes can be a marinade or baste; they can be used for both grilled and broiled foods. Prepare all sauces in a blender, or by hand as follows: Combine all ingredients in a small bowl. Whisk vigorously to blend.

Seasoned Italian

Use for chicken or turkey. Makes about 1½ cups.

    2 tomatoes, peeled, seeded, and puréed
   ½ cup olive oil
    2 tablespoons dried oregano
    1 clove garlic, minced
   ⅛ teaspoon salt
      Freshly ground black pepper

East Indian Curry

Use for chicken, turkey, or game hens. Makes about ½ cup.

- ¼ cup oil
- 3 tablespoons lemon juice
- 2 tablespoons curry
- 1 tablespoon apricot jam

Citrus-Cinnamon

Use for all poultry. Makes about 1 cup.

- ½ cup fresh orange juice
- ¼ cup oil
- 2 tablespoons orange-flavored liqueur
- ¼ teaspoon ground cinnamon

Japanese

Use for all poultry. Makes about ½ cup.

- ¼ cup sesame oil
- 3 tablespoons sherry
- 3 tablespoons rice wine vinegar
- 1 tablespoon freshly grated ginger

Red-Pepper Cajun

Use for chicken or turkey. This sauce is spicy, so marinate only 1 hour. Makes about 1 cup.

- ¾ cup dry red wine
- ¼ cup vegetable oil
- 3 tablespoons hot red-pepper sauce (not *Tabasco sauce*)
- 1 tablespoon prepared mustard

Honey-Mustard

Use for all poultry. Makes about ¾ cup.

- ½ cup honey
- ¼ cup water
- ½ teaspoon dry mustard

Lemon-Clove

Use for all poultry; especially good with pheasant. Makes about ¾ cup.

- ½ cup vegetable oil
- 2 tablespoons lemon juice
- 2 whole cloves
- 1 bay leaf
- ½ teaspoon sugar
- ⅛ teaspoon salt
  Pinch freshly ground black pepper

Sweet-and-Sour

For all poultry. Makes about 1½ cups.

- ½ cup soy sauce
- ½ cup pineapple juice
- ¼ cup oil
- 1 tablespoon brown sugar
- 2 teaspoons ground ginger
- 1 teaspoon dry mustard
- 1 clove garlic, crushed
- ¼ teaspoon freshly ground black pepper

Port Wine

For all poultry; very good with duck or pheasant. Makes about ¾ cup.

- ¼ cup each *vegetable oil, port wine, and orange juice*
- 1 teaspoon honey

The mild flavor of poultry adapts well to all manner of marinades and bastes, whether it's the sweetness of honey or brown sugar, the tartness of citrus, the pungency of herbs and spices, or the mellow richness of port wine.

SEPTEMBER CELEBRATION

Broiled Duck Breasts With Apricot-Mustard Glaze

Potatoes Anna

Tomatoes Stuffed With Peas

Pear Crumble With Almond Whipped Cream

Pinot Noir Blanc

Usher in the first cool night of autumn with elegant broiled duck glazed with mustard and apricot jam. Every dish in this menu can be assembled in advance— the Pear Crumble the day before, the stuffed tomatoes and Potatoes Anna the morning of the dinner party. All that's left is to quickly broil the duck breasts just before dinner is served.

BROILED DUCK BREASTS WITH APRICOT-MUSTARD GLAZE

2 whole ducks (about 4½ lbs each)
  Salt and freshly ground black pepper
1 clove garlic, slivered

Apricot-Mustard Glaze

½ cup apricot jam
3 tablespoons Dijon mustard
3 tablespoons soy sauce
3 tablespoons honey
1 clove garlic, minced

1. Wash ducks and pat dry. Remove innards. Bone ducks so that breasts are removed with skin attached. Reserve duck carcasses for stock and the duck legs for another recipe (they can be used for Chinese Duck Salad, page 122).

2. Split duck breasts to make 4 half-breasts. Remove visible fat from underside of skin. Season lightly with salt and pepper. Prick holes in skin covering the breasts and insert garlic slivers.

3. Prepare Apricot-Mustard Glaze. Brush glaze on both sides of breast halves.

4. Preheat broiler. Broil breast halves, skin side down, about 6 inches from heat for 6 minutes. Turn and broil 2 to 3 minutes more. Be careful not to burn duck.

5. To serve, slice breasts on the bias and serve with remaining Apricot-Mustard Glaze.

Serves 4.

Apricot-Mustard Glaze In a small bowl combine jam, mustard, soy sauce, honey, and minced garlic.

Makes about 1 cup.

POTATOES ANNA

2 tablespoons butter
2 tablespoons oil
3 cups peeled and thinly sliced potatoes
  Salt, freshly ground black pepper, and paprika

1. Preheat oven to 375° F. In an ovenproof skillet over medium heat, melt butter with oil. Remove skillet from heat.

2. Pat potato slices dry. Layer them in a slightly overlapping spiral pattern in butter and oil in bottom of skillet. Sprinkle with salt, pepper, and paprika. Repeat layers until all the potatoes are used, basting each layer with butter-oil mixture drawn from bottom of skillet (you can do this easily with a bulb baster).

3. Return skillet to heat. Cook potatoes over medium-high heat until they turn golden brown (about 10 minutes). Shake pan occasionally to keep potatoes from sticking.

4. Cover and set on middle rack of oven; bake until potatoes are heated through and tender, and butter is absorbed (about 30 minutes). Invert potatoes onto serving platter.

Serves 4.

TOMATOES STUFFED WITH PEAS

4 large, firm tomatoes
2 tablespoons butter
  Half an onion, minced
1 cup frozen peas
  Salt and freshly ground black pepper

1. Preheat oven to 375° F. Wash and dry tomatoes. With a sharp knife, slice top off each. Scoop out core and seeds. Turn shells upside down to drain.

2. In a medium skillet over medium heat, melt butter and sauté onion until translucent. Add frozen peas and heat until peas are just cooked through. Set aside.

3. Season inside of tomato shells with salt and pepper. Spoon onion-pea mixture into shells.

4. Place tomatoes in a greased oven-proof dish. Cover and set on middle rack of oven; bake until tomatoes are just tender (about 15 minutes).

Serves 4.

PEAR CRUMBLE WITH ALMOND WHIPPED CREAM

> 2 *pounds Comice pears*
> 3 *tablespoons granulated sugar*
> 2 *tablespoons brown sugar*

Topping

> 1½ *cups flour*
> 6 *tablespoons butter, cut in pieces*
> ¼ *cup granulated sugar*

Almond Whipped Cream

> 1 *cup whipping cream*
> 1 *teaspoon almond extract*

1. Preheat oven to 400° F. Peel, core, and slice pears; arrange in a greased 9- by 9-inch baking dish. Sprinkle with granulated sugar.

2. Prepare topping and spoon evenly over pears; press in lightly. Sprinkle brown sugar over top.

3. Place baking dish on middle rack of oven; bake until top is golden brown (about 35 minutes).

4. Prepare Almond Whipped Cream. Serve Pear Crumble with generous dollop of Almond Whipped Cream.

Serves 8 to 10.

Topping Sift flour into a medium bowl. Rub butter lightly into flour with fingertips. Mix in granulated sugar.

Almond Whipped Cream In a medium bowl combine cream and almond extract and whip with an electric mixer until stiff.

Makes 2 cups.

For your first dinner party of the fall season, consider this menu. Although the food is impressive, much of it can be prepared beforehand, leaving you free to be with your guests.

Tempura Chicken (see page 66) is a flavorful example of the appeal of deep-frying: succulent, moist meat inside a crispy brown exterior.

Sautéing, Stir-Frying & Deep-Frying

The three cooking methods discussed in this chapter are all variations on one of the most basic culinary techniques—rapid frying in hot fat over high heat. Frying is universally appreciated for the wonderful flavor and crisp, browned surface it produces. This chapter provides complete instructions and recipes for each of these techniques, plus tips on frying grease-free (see page 58), recipes for a stir-fry supper (see pages 60–61), and a Southern-style picnic featuring two recipes for fried chicken (see pages 68–71).

COOKING WITH FAT

Frying is part of almost every cuisine and a component of many cooking methods. Its appeal is in the wonderful flavor and crisp, browned surface of food cooked this way. It is particularly versatile, and when properly executed, it produces foods that are light and not at all greasy. Consider Chicken Kiev (page 66), Turkey Croquettes (page 66), Tempura Chicken (page 66), Country Fried Chicken (page 68), Chicken Breasts in Vermouth (page 57)—different applications of essentially the same process.

It is an approach well suited to cooking poultry; when cooked quickly at high heat, tender poultry retains natural juices and gains extra flavor. Using sautéing, stir-frying, or deep-frying, any cook can turn out an impressive meal in very little time. A boneless chicken breast, quickly cooked in a bit of sizzling fat to a golden brown finish, served with a sauce made of pan juices blended with wine or stock and selected herbs and spices, is a classically elegant dish. Start to finish, this succulent chicken sauté is ready in less than 30 minutes, and it will please the most particular palate. This is fast food in the best sense—flavorful, presentable, and easy on today's busy cook.

VARIATIONS ON A THEME

Sauté and stir-fry are the same technique, differentiated by national origin, typical ingredients, and type of pan used. *Sautéing* comes from the classic French tradition, tends to creamy sauces and few vegetables, and is done in the sauté pan, essentially a frying pan; *stir-frying* is a technique most common in Oriental cooking, usually involving a number of vegetables and no dairy products, and employs a wok. *Deep-frying* involves total immersion of food in fat. Technically, there is also a fourth category of frying, *pan-frying*, which is halfway between sautéing and deep-frying. Pan-fried foods are first dipped in a flour or crumb coating, then cooked in an inch or so of hot fat. But sautéing, stir-frying, and deep-frying are the most commonly used techniques and therefore the focus of this chapter. Regardless of terminology, the goal for all of these methods is the same: brown, crisp, evenly cooked food, quickly prepared.

Only young poultry is suitable for frying. This technique does not take long enough to tenderize older, tougher birds. For all frying methods, poultry must be cut in uniformly sized pieces, or be thin or small enough to cook through in a short time. Very small whole birds, such as quail, can be successfully fried.

Frying is an active, fast-moving cooking method that demands concentration and quick responses. The cook must be alert to changes both in the food, as it changes from raw to cooked, and in the hot fat. Even a slight hesitation can make the difference between brown or burned, tender or tough poultry.

Which Method to Use?

Choice of method is often determined by what's on hand to cook with and the amount of preparation time available. Sautéed dishes are perhaps the simplest to put together. For a basic sauté, all that is needed is tender, cut-up poultry, a liquid to make the sauce, and seasonings. You'll want to pound boned poultry to a uniform thickness, but otherwise no preparation is needed. Deep-fried chicken also calls for a minimum of ingredients—perhaps just a coating—and time. Stir-frying, although equally quick and simple, entails the most preparation. Poultry and other ingredients must be cut to proper size; sauce ingredients should be portioned out and ready; marinades must be mixed and applied well ahead of cooking. Chopping, cutting, and some marinating can be done early in the day, or the night before. Each of these methods is simplified with some planning and a well-stocked pantry and refrigerator.

FATS, OILS, AND TEMPERATURE

The high heat of frying rapidly cooks tender cuts of meat, sears their surfaces, retains moisture, and promotes browning. For all of the frying methods, fats and oils are the media by which heat is transferred to food. With a boiling point higher than water, fats and oils cook hotter, and therefore faster, than other liquids. Because heated fat caramelizes sugars in the food, it encourages the characteristic browned surface on fried foods. Fat also keeps food from sticking to the pan.

SOME CAUTIONS ON COOKING WITH OIL

Hot oil is dangerous. And any oil that has been heated is hot oil. If left unattended over heat, it can eventually reach its fire point and burst into flame. Should this happen, smother the fire with the pan cover and remove from the heat. Baking soda and salt will also put out a grease fire, but do not attempt to douse it with water, which will only spread the flames further. It's wise to equip your kitchen with a fire extinguisher designed for grease fires.

Hot oil can also burn the careless cook. Turn the pot handle away from you, over the stove rather than projecting into the room, so that it cannot be accidentally bumped, spilling the scalding fat.

HOW TO CHOOSE AN OIL

When frying, it is most important to use a fat that will stay intact at high heat. Eventually, any fat or oil will become hot enough to decompose.

The point at which this breakdown occurs is called the *smoke point*. At this stage, smoke and an acrid gas are given off, the liquid begins to darken, and an unpleasant taste is imparted to food. Oils with high smoke points include safflower oil, grapeseed oil, corn oil, and peanut oil. Lard and solid vegetable shortening are also sometimes used. Sesame and olive oils, with lower smoke points, are less suitable for frying, and work better as seasonings.

An oil's smoke point is lowered each time the fat is reused. After it has been used three or four times, it must be discarded. Bits of food afloat in the oil will also accelerate this breakdown. It is important to continually skim off crumbs from the hot oil, and to strain used oil through cheesecloth before storing. Exposure to air will also lower the smoke point. For this reason, a narrow, deep pot is preferable to a shallow, wide pan when a great deal of fat is used, as in deep-frying.

Select an oil that is appropriate to the recipe. An oil with a mild or neutral taste will not mask the flavor of the food. A stronger oil, such as peanut oil, imparts its own flavor and is used where this would be desirable, such as in stir-frying.

FRYING TEMPERATURE

Not only is it critical that you choose a fat that will stand up to high temperature, but you also need to maintain this high heat throughout the cooking process. Fluctuating temperature will result in poultry that is either overdone on the outside and raw in the middle, or bland and greasy. An electric skillet or fryer with a built-in thermostat will monitor temperature changes and correct for them automatically. However, with any other frying method, the cook will need to evaluate the cooking process and adjust the heat or the food as necessary. A deep-fat thermometer will help by indicating tem-
(continued on page 55)

Sautés, like Chicken Breasts in Vermouth (see page 57), look complicated but are actually quick to put together. The special appeal of this dish is the rich vermouth cream sauce, flavored with grated orange rind.

COATINGS

In general, a coating acts as a protective barrier between the oil and the food. Because deep-fried foods come into contact with more fat than those that are sautéed or stir-fried, there is a greater chance of overabsorption of the fat. The cook can prevent overabsorption by maintaining the proper cooking temperature and by sealing the poultry with a coating.

Coatings also improve the taste, appearance, and texture of fried poultry. There are three ways to coat poultry: breading with a "bound" coating, dredging with flour or cornstarch, and coating with a batter.

Breading

This process utilizes a "bound" coating of flour, the binder—beaten egg (often with some water or milk added to extend the liquid)—and bread crumbs. Flour dries the outside of the poultry pieces and gives the egg something to adhere to; without the flour base, egg has a tendency to peel away during frying. The egg acts as a glue to hold the layer of bread crumbs. The crumbs add texture and color. A bound coating must set for at least 30 minutes to dry out the egg. (This resting period allows the cook to prepare other dishes or start cleanup.) Breaded food can also be held in the refrigerator overnight if necessary, and then brought back to room temperature 30 minutes before cooking. Although best when served immediately, breaded poultry can be kept warm in a slow (200° F) oven for up to two hours. Do not let the poultry pieces touch during this time or they will steam and get soggy.

BREAD COATING FOR POULTRY

½ cup flour
1 egg, lightly beaten
½ to ¾ cup dry bread crumbs

Sprinkle the flour on a plate or large square of waxed paper. Have the beaten egg in a deep dish, such as a pie plate. The bread crumbs should be on a plate or large square of waxed paper. Dip the poultry pieces in each ingredient in the order given, then let pieces sit at room temperature for 30 minutes before cooking.

Makes enough to cover 1½ pounds of poultry.

Dredging

Dusting with flour or cornstarch (sometimes seasoned) is the simplest method of coating. The powdery finish ensures that the surface of food to be fried is dry (moisture is to be avoided because it causes hot oil to sputter and drop in temperature, and because wet food steams instead of fries and won't brown properly). Dredging is most commonly used for sautéing and stir-frying. Deep-fried foods are better protected by a more substantial covering, such as a batter or breading, which will also impart a crisper texture and better flavor.

SEASONED FLOUR

½ cup flour
1 teaspoon salt
1 teaspoon freshly ground black pepper
2 teaspoons paprika
2 teaspoons fines herbes

Mix all ingredients together in a bag or pie plate. Put poultry pieces in bag and toss to cover with seasoned flour, or dredge pieces in pie plate.

Makes enough to cover 1½ pounds of poultry.

Batters

A batter is composed of flour mixed with liquid, such as milk, wine, or beer, and a leavening agent, often eggs or egg whites, yeast, or baking powder. Batters have a wonderful taste, but are not as convenient as dredging or breading. They must rest in the refrigerator for two to three hours before use to allow the flour to blend completely with the liquid, to give the leavening a chance to activate, and to allow the gluten to relax. Without this resting time, the batter will pull off of the food. Batter-frying is a messy process, and one that allows little time between setup and cooking—once a food has been dipped in the batter, it cannot be put down or the coating will come off; it must be cooked immediately.

BATTER FOR POULTRY

1⅓ cups flour
1 teaspoon salt
¼ teaspoon freshly ground black pepper
1 tablespoon oil
2 egg yolks, lightly beaten
1¼ cups flat beer
2 egg whites, beaten until stiff

1. In a medium bowl mix together flour, salt, pepper, oil, egg yolks, and beer. Cover and refrigerate for at least 3 hours.

2. When ready to use, fold egg whites into batter. Dip pieces of poultry in batter and fry immediately.

Makes enough to cover 1½ pounds of poultry.

perature variations. Experienced cooks often depend on their senses, in addition to a thermometer, to judge when a fat is hot enough to use.

For deep-fat frying, drop a cube of bread into the hot oil and slowly count to 60. If the bread has browned nicely, the oil is ready. If the bread has burned, the oil is too hot. If the bread stays pale and becomes saturated with fat, the oil is not hot enough.

For sautéing with butter or a butter-and-oil combination, watch for the butter to foam. Unclarified butter is quick to burn, so it must be watched carefully. With butter you can also be alert to the *point of fragrance*—the moment at which its characteristic aroma becomes apparent.

For all methods, the familiar sizzle when food meets hot fat is yet another indicator that proper frying temperature has been reached.

FRYING TECHNIQUE

Poultry and other ingredients (with a very few exceptions) should be at room temperature at the time of cooking. Cold food will immediately lower the temperature of the fat to below an optimum level. If food must be fried before it has warmed to approximately 70° F, cook only a few pieces at a time.

The surface of the poultry pieces should be as dry as possible. Pat poultry dry with a paper towel, or coat it with flour, a breading, or a batter. Any surface moisture will instantly convert to steam as it meets the hot fat, causing the fat to bubble up and possibly overflow the sides of the pan, as well as bringing about an immediate drop in temperature. Overcrowding the pan will also produce excess moisture. Frying too many pieces of food at one time will steam, not brown, what's being cooked. Between batches, always allow the oil to return to the proper temperature.

SAUTÉING: ELEGANT AND EASY

A cook who understands the art of sautéing can quickly put together delicious, always presentable fare in very little time. Usually, minimal preparation is needed, as long as the pantry is appropriately stocked. This cooking method is so versatile, appealing, and easy that a different poultry sauté could be prepared every night for a month without boring either cook or guest.

Sautéing has been done for centuries, with the French and Chinese its most accomplished practitioners. The term itself comes from the French *sauter*, meaning "to jump." In its strictest culinary application, small, uniformly sized pieces of food are rapidly cooked over high heat in oil

For Quail in Red Wine (see page 58), the birds are sautéed, then topped with a wine-and-stock sauce made with pan drippings and served with Garlic Toast—a dramatic opener for a company dinner.

Cheese-Crusted Chicken (see page 59) is fried chicken with a difference. Boned chicken breasts are coated with seasoned flour, grated mild cheese, and bread crumbs, then sautéed to a golden brown. The speed of the cooking keeps the meat juicy.

or fat in a specially designed, straight-sided, shallow pan with an extra-long handle. To keep the food from sticking, the pan is kept in constant motion, so the food "jumps" in the pan. More typically, sautéed food is turned, rather than tossed. Any skillet made of a material that conducts heat well can be substituted for a sauté pan.

When the food is browned on all sides, it is removed from the pan and kept warm while the juices are made into an accompanying sauce. *Deglazing* removes caramelized bits of food from the bottom of the pan and incorporates them into the liquid that is the base for the sauce. To deglaze the pan, set the sautéed meat aside. If there is more than a thin film of fat in the pan, discard the excess. Pour a clear liquid, such as stock, wine, or

brandy, into the pan and cook over high heat, scraping the bottom of the pan to loosen drippings into the liquid. From this point, a sauce can be made. It can be elementary—a mix of fresh lemon juice and stock—or rich with whipping cream and grated cheeses. Other successful combinations include: dry red wine, stock, and capers; white wine, mushrooms, and shallots; brandy, cream, and green onions; or red wine, chopped tomatoes, and Provençale herbs (see pages 102–109 for more about sauces). As you become comfortable with this method, you will be inspired to create your own sautés and sauces.

If dinner must be prepared and then held, sautéed poultry will keep in a warm oven (200° F) for up to two hours, uncovered. The accompanying sauce can be made just before serving, or up to two hours in advance. Let the sauce sit in a covered pan until needed, and then gently reheat.

GETTING STARTED

As with all dry-heat cooking, sautéing requires tender cuts of poultry. Usually any cut suitable for grilling or broiling can also be sautéed. Poultry pieces that are to be cooked in the same pan must be uniform in size and shape; if necessary, use a meat pounder to achieve an even thickness. Dark meat, which takes longer to cook, should be put in the pan first and cooked for a short time, and then the white meat added.

Make sure that the poultry is as dry as possible, so that it will brown quickly. Keep the pan moving to prevent food from sticking; use a spatula to free any pieces that do adhere. Drain cooked food over the pan and then on paper towels. Follow the frying guidelines in "Fats, Oils, and Temperature," pages 52-55.

Oil alone, or butter and oil in a ratio of 2 parts butter to 1 part oil, is the usual choice for sautéing poultry. Many cooks like to use at least some butter for its flavor. Butter burns, however, so either it must be clarified or it must be blended with oil to raise its smoke point.

CHICKEN BREASTS IN VERMOUTH

This dish, elegant enough for guests, looks impressive, but it actually couldn't be easier to put together. As with all sautés, it will hold in a 200° F oven for up to two hours, uncovered. The vermouth-cream sauce, with its hint of orange, can stay covered at room temperature just as long. Reheat any sauce over very low heat to prevent separation. Serve the dish with souffléed potatoes and a steamed vegetable to round out the menu.

3 *whole chicken breasts, halved, boned, and skinned*
3 *tablespoons oil*
1 *clove garlic, minced*
1 *shallot, minced*
¾ *cup dry vermouth*
¼ *pound mushrooms, sliced*
1 *cup whipping cream*
   Salt and freshly ground black pepper
1 *egg yolk*
1 *tablespoon grated orange rind*

1. Preheat oven to 200° F. Wash breast halves and pat dry.

2. In a medium, heavy-bottomed skillet over medium heat, heat oil with garlic. Sauté breast halves in the oil until browned on both sides (about 5 to 7 minutes per side).

3. Remove breasts to an ovenproof serving dish, draining as much of the oil as possible into the skillet. Keep breasts warm, uncovered, in oven while you prepare sauce.

4. Add shallot to skillet and sauté until brown. Pour in the vermouth, scraping the pan drippings and any browned bits from the bottom and side of pan. Simmer until liquid is reduced to about half the original volume. Add mushrooms and quickly heat through. Pour in cream, increase heat to high, and bring to a boil to thicken. Reduce heat to low. Season with salt and pepper.

5. Put egg yolk into a small bowl. Stir in about ¼ cup of the hot sauce. Pour this mixture back into skillet and simmer until sauce thickens. Do not boil, or egg yolk will curdle. Add orange rind and simmer briefly, stirring to blend.

6. Pour the sauce over the chicken and serve.

Serves 6.

THE SAUTÉ PANTRY

If the simplicity and speed of sautéing appeal to you, consider having the following on hand as staples in your refrigerator and pantry.

In the refrigerator
Butter (including clarified butter), cream or half-and-half, eggs, sauce bases, stock. Freeze stock and sauce bases held longer than a few days.

On the shelf *Bread crumbs, flour, herbs and spices, oils, canned tomatoes and tomato purée, red and white wine, sherry, brandy.*

Equipment *Sauté pan or skillet, wooden spoons, slotted spoons, spatula, meat pounder, paper towels.*

HOW TO FRY GREASE-FREE

Deep-fried poultry can be greasy if improperly prepared. To reduce the amount of fat the poultry absorbs, set up a barrier—a coating of some kind—between the fat and the food. Then cook the poultry quickly: The less time it must spend in the oil, the less greasy it will be. To produce a light, flavorful, crisp, browned piece of poultry each time you fry, remember to:

☐ *Have the oil hot enough that the poultry will sear immediately and cook quickly.*

☐ *Make sure the poultry is dry, then protect it with a coating, such as flour, bread crumbs, or a batter.*

☐ *Use a wire fry basket or a slotted spoon to drain excess fat from cooked poultry into the pan.*

☐ *Drain fried poultry on paper towels before serving.*

CINNAMON CHICKEN MEATBALLS

These pan-fried meatballs can be eaten with toothpicks as an appetizer, or you can serve them as a main course accompanied with eggplant slices sautéed in garlic oil and a bulgur pilaf made with raisins and pine nuts.

    ½ cup dry bread crumbs
    ½ cup milk
    1½ pounds ground raw chicken
    ½ cup minced green onion
        (including green portion)
    2 cloves garlic, crushed
    1 teaspoon ground cinnamon
    ½ teaspoon salt
    ½ teaspoon freshly ground black
       pepper
    ½ cup flour
    1 cup clarified butter (see
       opposite page)

1. Soak bread crumbs in milk and set aside.

2. In a medium bowl combine chicken, green onion, garlic, cinnamon, salt, and pepper. With hands, thoroughly mix in soaked bread crumbs. Chill mixture, covered, for at least 3 hours.

3. Set flour on a large square of waxed paper. Shape chicken into 3-inch balls. Roll in flour, shake off excess, and set aside on rack or plate.

4. In a medium, heavy-bottomed skillet over medium heat, melt clarified butter. Add meatballs and sauté until golden brown all around (about 5 to 7 minutes).

5. Serve hot as an appetizer or main course.

Makes about 30 meatballs.

QUAIL IN RED WINE

Small game birds are perfect first courses. Serve these quail on pieces of garlic toast, and encourage guests to use the toast to finish any sauce that remains on the plate.

    6 quail
    ½ cup plus 2 tablespoons flour
    1 teaspoon salt
    ¼ cup butter
    ¼ cup sliced onion
    ¼ cup Chicken Stock (see
       page 91)
    ¼ cup red wine
    ¼ cup sliced mushrooms

Garlic Toast

    ¼ cup butter
    1 clove garlic, crushed
    12 slices French bread

1. Preheat oven to 200° F. Warm serving platter in oven while oven preheats. Wash quail and pat dry.

2. Sift the ½ cup flour with salt onto a large square of waxed paper. Dredge quail in flour.

3. In a medium, heavy-bottomed skillet over medium heat, melt butter. Add quail and sauté until golden brown (about 10 minutes per side). Remove to warm platter in oven.

4. Add onion to skillet and sauté until translucent. Stir in the 2 tablespoons flour and cook until golden. Add stock and wine. Simmer, stirring constantly, until smooth and velvety. Add mushrooms and cook through.

5. Return quail to skillet, drizzle with sauce, and heat through. In another skillet, prepare Garlic Toast.

6. To serve, place 2 pieces of Garlic Toast on each plate, top with 1 quail, and spoon sauce over all.

Serves 6.

Garlic Toast In a skillet over medium-high heat, melt butter. Add garlic and sauté briefly (do not brown). Lightly brown bread slices on both sides in garlic butter (about 2 minutes per side).

Makes 12 pieces of toast.

CHEESE-CRUSTED CHICKEN

A perfect picnic dish because it is as good cold as it is hot, this chicken sauté does not require a sauce. Its flavor is in its coating of flour, bread crumbs, and Swiss cheese. Have a spatula nearby while the breasts are browning—as the cheese coating melts, it may stick to the pan.

  2 whole chicken breasts, halved, boned, and skinned
1¼ cups flour
  ½ teaspoon salt
  ⅛ teaspoon ground nutmeg
  ⅛ teaspoon pepper
  1 egg, lightly beaten
  ⅔ cup grated Swiss, Gruyère, or Emmenthaler cheese
  ½ cup dry bread crumbs
  ¼ cup butter
  1 lemon, cut in wedges, for garnish

1. Wash breast halves and pat dry. Pound between two sheets of waxed paper to ¼-inch thickness. Set aside.

2. Sift flour, salt, nutmeg, and pepper onto a large square of waxed paper. Set aside. Have beaten egg in a pie pan. Mix together cheese and bread crumbs and set aside on a large square of waxed paper or a plate.

3. Coat breast halves with seasoned flour, shaking off excess. Dip in egg, then in cheese-crumb mixture, coating well.

4. In a large, heavy-bottomed skillet over medium heat, melt butter. Add chicken and sauté until golden brown on both sides (about 5 minutes per side). Drain on paper towels. Serve with lemon wedges.

Serves 4.

TURKEY MARSALA

The sauté Marsala is a classic, often done with veal or chicken. The cutlets need to be quite thin; you may want to ask your butcher to flatten them for you.

1½ pounds turkey cutlets
  ½ cup plus 2 tablespoons flour
  ¼ cup butter
  1 tablespoon oil
  ½ cup Marsala wine
  ½ cup Chicken Stock (see page 91)
      Salt and freshly ground black pepper
      Sprigs of parsley, for garnish

1. Preheat oven to 200° F. Warm serving platter in oven while oven preheats. Wash turkey cutlets; pat dry.

2. If your butcher has not flattened the cutlets, pound them between two sheets of waxed paper to ⅛-inch thickness. Dredge in the ½ cup flour to coat; shake off excess flour. Set cutlets aside.

3. In a large, heavy-bottomed skillet over medium heat, melt 2 tablespoons of the butter with oil. Add cutlets and sauté until golden brown on both sides (about 2 minutes per side). Remove to warm platter in oven.

4. Pour Marsala into skillet and simmer for 2 minutes, scraping pan drippings and any browned bits from bottom and sides of pan. Pour Marsala and pan juices into small bowl and reserve.

5. Melt the remaining 2 tablespoons butter in skillet over medium-high heat. Stir in the 2 tablespoons flour and cook until golden (about 2 minutes). Add Chicken Stock and reserved Marsala, whisking continuously until sauce is smooth and velvety. Season with salt and pepper.

6. Add turkey to sauce and coat evenly. Garnish with parsley sprigs.

Serves 4.

CLARIFIED BUTTER

Clarifying butter removes the milk solids that burn when butter is heated. What remains is a clear yellow liquid able to withstand high heat. It has a clearer taste than whole butter and is preferred for light sauces and for quick-cooking delicate poultry and fish.

Clarified butter is costly because you lose about half the butter's original volume. It does keep almost indefinitely in the refrigerator (ghee, widely used in the Middle East and the Orient, is clarified butter stored at room temperature).

To clarify butter: In a 2-quart double boiler, melt 1 pound of butter over medium-high heat. Allow the butter to foam. Stir, then reduce the heat until the foam subsides. Let the butter foam again, stir, and remove from the heat. Let the butter stand for 30 minutes. Pour off the clear yellow liquid on top and store. Discard the milky residue that remains in the pan.

Makes 1 cup.

STIR-FRY SUPPER

Moo Goo Gai Pan

Rice Vermicelli

Gingered Vegetables

Almond Float

Japanese or Chinese Beer

Chinese meals are often complicated to orchestrate. Many ingredients require advance preparation and most dishes must be cooked at the last minute. A realistic approach to such meals is to limit the number of stir-fried dishes to one or two. Remember to allow refrigerated ingredients to return to room temperature before cooking. Rice vermicelli and canned lichee nuts are available in the Oriental foods section of many supermarkets or at specialty food stores.

MOO GOO GAI PAN

  3 whole chicken breasts, halved, boned, and skinned
      Salt and freshly ground black pepper
  ⅓ cup oil
  3 slices fresh ginger
  2 cloves garlic
 1½ cups Chicken Stock (see page 91)
  2 tablespoons cornstarch
  ½ pound mushrooms, sliced
  ¼ pound snow peas, trimmed
  1 can (8 oz) water chestnuts, drained and sliced
  4 green onions, julienned
  2 to 3 tablespoons soy sauce

1. Wash chicken and pat dry. Slice into strips 1½ inches long and ¼ inch wide. Season lightly with salt and pepper. Set aside.

2. Preheat wok over high heat for 1 minute. Swirl oil around sides of pan. When oil is hot, add ginger and garlic, brown, then discard.

3. Add chicken pieces to wok. Stir-fry over high heat for about 4 minutes, stirring to coat with oil.

4. Combine Chicken Stock and cornstarch. Pour over chicken and reduce heat. Add mushrooms, snow peas, water chestnuts, and green onions. Stir to coat with liquid. Cover wok and simmer until done (about 10 to 15 minutes).

5. Season with soy sauce and serve immediately.

Serves 6.

RICE VERMICELLI

 10 cups water
  2 teaspoons salt
  6 ounces rice vermicelli
  1 teaspoon oil

1. In a 4-quart saucepan bring water to a boil with salt. Add vermicelli and oil, stir, and return to a boil. Cook until just tender (about 5 minutes).

2. Drain in a colander. Keep warm in saucepan until ready to serve.

Makes 3 cups.

GINGERED VEGETABLES

 1 to 2 tablespoons oil
  1 slice fresh ginger
  2 ribs celery, sliced diagonally
  1 small carrot, peeled and sliced diagonally
      Half a head broccoli, tops cut into florets, stems julienned
  1 green onion, julienned
  1 package (1 oz) shiitake mushrooms, soaked according to package directions, then sliced
  ½ cup Chicken Stock (see page 91)
  1 tablespoon cornstarch mixed with 2 tablespoons water
 1 to 2 tablespoons soy sauce

1. Preheat wok over high heat for 1 minute. Swirl oil around sides of pan. Add ginger; brown; discard. Add celery, carrot, broccoli, and green onion; stir-fry constantly. When vegetables are just tender, add mushrooms.

2. Pour in stock, cover, and simmer 10 minutes. Add cornstarch paste, stirring to blend. Season with soy sauce and serve immediately.

Serves 6.

ALMOND FLOAT

  1 tablespoon (1 envelope) unflavored gelatin
  ⅓ cup cold water
  ¾ cup boiling water
  ⅓ cup sugar
  1 cup milk
  1 teaspoon almond extract
  1 can (20 oz) lichee nuts, drained and syrup reserved

1. Soften gelatin in the cold water and pour into a medium saucepan. Add the boiling water and sugar; stir over low heat until sugar and gelatin are dissolved. Pour in milk and almond extract. Stir to blend.

2. Pour mixture into an 8-inch square baking pan and chill until firm (about 4 hours).

3. To serve, turn out and cut into diamonds. Serve with lichee nuts. Drizzle with lichee syrup.

Serves 6.

Chicken stir-fried with fresh vegetables and water chestnuts is the star of this menu. Much of the meal can be prepared up to a day ahead.

Spicy Tangerine Chicken (see page 64) is first marinated, then quickly stir-fried and served with a hot and tangy sauce made right in the wok.

STIR-FRYING: FAST AND FLAVORFUL

Sautéing and stir-frying are basically the same technique; the difference between them is primarily cultural. Stir-fried dishes, reflecting the Chinese palate, include many vegetables. Dairy products, so important in French sauce making, are not used.

The cooking pan, a wok, is round-bottomed and requires less oil than does a sauté pan or skillet. Less fat means that stir-fried dishes have fewer calories than other fried foods. Each piece of meat or vegetable gets immersed in the small pool of oil that collects in the wok's bowl and is quickly seared and cooked. The result, as devotees of Oriental cuisine have always known, is extremely flavorful and fresh-tasting. Vegetables retain their natural color; poultry remains moist and tender. Poultry plays a versatile role in Chinese cooking, tasting remarkably different from recipe to recipe. Its subtle taste is an excellent foil to sauces.

Stir-frying is as simple to execute as other frying methods, but it is usually complex in preparation. Typical ingredients can be difficult to find outside of areas where there are large Asian populations. Its necessary speed requires that chopping and slicing be done in advance, sauces and spices premeasured, thickening agents blended.

To smooth the preparation, shop for and ready all the ingredients a day ahead. About 30 minutes before cooking, remove them from the refrigerator and allow them to come to room temperature.

HOW TO USE A WOK

A wok's sloping sides allow a small amount of oil to cook a significant amount of food. As opposed to other pan-frying methods where the fat and pan heat together, a wok must be preheated before any oil is added. This preheating prevents food from sticking to the wok's sides. Oil is added in swirls starting near the upper edge of the inside of the pan. The oil runs to the bottom, coating the wok's interior surface. Pieces of food are then quickly tossed in the hot oil. If ingredients require different cooking times, they are stir-fried separately and set aside. Sauce ingredients are blended in toward the end of cooking and heated until thickened. All ingredients are then returned to the wok, heated through, and coated with sauce.

Use an oil that holds a high heat, such as grapeseed oil. Peanut oil, frequently recommended for stir-frying, will add extra flavor. To proceed, follow the general frying guidelines in the section entitled "Fats, Oils, and Temperature" (pages 52–55).

ALMOND CHICKEN

Oriental dishes are often categorized by their place of origin. This recipe, from the Chinese city of Canton, is a familiar Cantonese preparation. It can be doubled.

- 1 whole chicken breast, halved, boned, and skinned
- 3 tablespoons oil
- ½ cup diced celery
- ½ cup snow peas, trimmed
- 1 package (1 oz) dried shiitake mushrooms, soaked according to package directions
- 2 tablespoons soy sauce
- 1 teaspoon salt
- ¼ teaspoon freshly ground black pepper
- 1 tablespoon cornstarch mixed with 2 tablespoons water
- ¼ cup almonds

1. Wash chicken breast and pat dry. Slice into strips 1 inch long and ½ inch wide.

2. Preheat wok over high heat 1 minute. Swirl oil around sides of pan.

When oil is hot, add chicken fry until white and firm (ab minutes). Add celery, snow mushrooms, soy sauce, salt, and pepper; stir-fry 1 minute.

3. Add cornstarch paste, stirring to blend and thicken.

4. Mix in almonds and stir-fry to heat through (about 3 minutes). Serve immediately.

Serves 2.

SWEET-AND-SOUR CHICKEN

Honey is the unusual sweetener in this dish, which can be doubled.

- 1 whole chicken breast, halved, boned, and skinned
- 1 can (8¼ oz) unsweetened pineapple chunks
- 2 tablespoons cornstarch
- 1 tablespoon oil
- 2 tablespoons pale dry sherry
- 1 tablespoon honey
- 1 tablespoon rice wine vinegar
- 1 tablespoon soy sauce
- 1 can (8 oz) water chestnuts, drained
- ¼ pound snow peas, trimmed

1. Wash chicken and pat dry. Cut into ½-inch cubes and set aside.

2. Drain pineapple chunks, reserve juice, and set pineapple aside. Blend pineapple juice with cornstarch and set aside.

3. Preheat wok over high heat for 1 minute. Swirl oil around sides of pan. When oil is hot, add chicken and stir-fry until white and firm (about 2 minutes). Add sherry, honey, vinegar, and soy sauce. Stir-fry 1 minute.

4. Add water chestnuts, snow peas, and reserved pineapple. Stir-fry 1 minute.

5. Add pineapple juice–cornstarch mixture and cook until thickened (about 1 minute). Serve immediately.

Serves 2.

THE STIR-FRY PANTRY

Ingredients for stir-fried dishes are not always easy to find. Try a well-stocked supermarket; they frequently have an ethnic foods section where many ingredients used for Oriental cooking can be found. If you are fortunate enough to have access to Oriental markets, your shopping will be simplified and the range of dishes you can prepare much expanded.

In the refrigerator
Snow peas, fresh ginger, fresh garlic, green onions, chicken stock. If you wish to hold stock longer than a few days, freeze it.

On the shelf *Dried mushrooms, canned bamboo shoots, canned water chestnuts, soy sauce, oyster sauce, hoisin sauce, hot-pepper sauce, peanut oil, sesame oil, rice wine, rice wine vinegar, pale dry sherry, cornstarch. (Most of these ingredients can be stored for a long time without refrigeration.)*

Equipment *Wok with cover, wooden spoons, slotted spoon.*

SPICY TANGERINE CHICKEN

Regulate the sauce's peppery bite by using more or less red pepper flakes according to personal preference. Note that the chicken needs to marinate at least eight hours.

> 1 egg white
> 1 tablespoon rice wine or pale dry sherry
> 1 tablespoon cornstarch
> 1 pound boneless skinned chicken meat, cut into ½-inch cubes
> ½ cup thinly sliced green onion (including green portion)
> 2 tablespoons minced fresh ginger
> 2 tablespoons minced garlic
> 1 tablespoon grated tangerine rind
> ½ teaspoon red pepper flakes
> ½ cup Chicken Stock (see page 91)
> 2 tablespoons soy sauce
> 2 tablespoons pale dry sherry
> 2 tablespoons rice wine vinegar
> 2 tablespoons sugar
> ⅓ cup oil
> 1 tablespoon cornstarch mixed with 2 tablespoons chicken stock

1. In a small bowl combine egg white, rice wine or sherry, and cornstarch and whisk until well mixed. Pour marinade over chicken pieces and refrigerate at least 8 hours.

2. In a small bowl combine green onion, ginger, garlic, tangerine rind, and red pepper flakes. Set aside.

3. In another small bowl combine stock, soy sauce, sherry, vinegar, and sugar. Stir to dissolve sugar. Set aside.

4. Preheat wok over high heat for 1 minute. Remove chicken from marinade; discard marinade. Swirl 3 tablespoons of the oil around sides of pan. When oil is hot, add chicken and stir-fry until partially cooked (1 to 2 minutes). Remove with a slotted spoon and set aside.

5. Heat remaining oil in wok for about 1 minute. Add onion-garlic-ginger mixture and stir-fry over medium-high heat until fragrant. Add chicken-stock mixture and simmer,

stirring frequently, until heated through (about 2 minutes). Add chicken and cook until white and firm (about 4 minutes).

6. Reduce heat to low. Mix in cornstarch paste and stir until sauce has a glossy finish. Serve immediately.

Serves 4.

CHICKEN WITH HOISIN SAUCE

Toast almonds in a dry skillet over medium-high heat, shaking pan occasionally, until a nutty aroma rises from the pan, three to four minutes.

> 2 whole chicken breasts, halved, boned, and skinned
> 1 tablespoon cornstarch
> 1 tablespoon pale dry sherry
> 1 tablespoon soy sauce
> ¼ cup oil
> 1 green pepper, cut in ½-inch squares
> 6 water chestnuts, drained and quartered
> ¼ pound mushrooms, quartered
> ¼ cup Chicken Stock (see page 91)
> 2 tablespoons hoisin sauce
> ¼ cup toasted whole almonds

1. Wash chicken, pat dry, and cut into ½-inch cubes. Place in a medium bowl and toss with cornstarch. Add sherry and soy sauce; toss again.

2. Preheat wok over high heat for 1 minute. Swirl 1 tablespoon of the oil around sides of pan. When oil is hot, add green pepper, water chestnuts, and mushrooms. Stir-fry about 3 minutes. Remove with a slotted spoon and set aside.

3. Swirl remaining oil around sides of wok and heat until fragrant (1 to 2 minutes). Add chicken pieces and stir-fry over high heat until chicken is white and firm (about 4 minutes). Add stock and hoisin sauce and stir to coat chicken. Add vegetables and cook 1 minute more, tossing to coat chicken with sauce. Add almonds and stir to heat through.

Serves 4.

As with all braises and stews, the flavor of Poulet Tangiers (see page 78) actually improves if the dish is made ahead and slowly reheated at serving time.

Stewing, Braising & Poaching

The family of liquid-cooked poultry dishes—stews, braises, fricassees, and poached foods— is notable for flavor, tenderness, and ease of preparation. The techniques differ from one another chiefly in the amount of liquid used: in poaching, the bird is completely immersed, stews and fricassees call for a moderate submersion, and braises take the least liquid. The recipes in this chapter include delicious examples of each type, such as Poussin Paprikash, a fricassee that is the centerpiece of a Hungarian dinner (see pages 82-83).

COOKING WITH LIQUID

When composing a menu, chefs and restaurateurs recognize that the names they give their specialties can make a difference to restaurant patrons. Homely "Chicken Stew With Vegetables" sounds too plain to be tempting. On the other hand, offer "Poule au Pot" or "Chicken Gumbo" or "Coq au Vin," all chicken-and-vegetable-stew variations, and you will be praised for your country-style cooking. Stews have an image problem, perhaps the result of over-starched and underflavored combinations sometimes prepared by uncaring cooks, or a reputation as "make do" meals, repositories for otherwise unworthy ingredients. Yet on a bone-chilling winter evening, few of us can resist the earthy appeal of poultry, vegetables, fragrant herbs, and rich stock gently simmering on the stove. And for busy cooks, these dishes are made to order, since they actually improve if made ahead and reheated.

Poultry stews and their extended family of liquid-based dishes, which includes braises, fricassees, and poached foods, are comforting, soul-warming, and satisfying. They have nurtured the peoples of the world for centuries and appear in almost every cuisine. These one-pot concoctions were born out of the need of thrifty peasant and pioneer cooks to extract every bit of nourishment and flavor from sometimes tough and tired ingredients. The slow stewing process required little attention once the dish was assembled, which freed the cook to attend to other chores. Like the patchwork quilts of the American prairie, these dishes were composed of leftovers, and when prepared with a talented hand, became art.

Today, creative American chefs and home cooks are rediscovering these robust dishes as they explore ethnic cooking for new ideas and new flavor combinations. The process of slow cooking in liquid is appreciated for the flavor it produces, even if we can now afford to use more tender frying or roasting chickens instead of tough old hens that required hours of simmering before they were fit to chew. When prepared with fresh ingredients and an adventuresome spirit, stews and their kin are lively, sensual, and always satisfying.

MOIST HEAT: RAPID AND RELIABLE

Stews, braises, and poached foods are heated by constantly moving currents of hot water and steam, similar to the circulating molecules of hot air that constitute dry heat. Liquids and steam, however, are more efficient conductors of heat than air. Food reaches an equilibrium of temperature both on its surface and at its center faster, and maintains it better, when cooked with moist heat. In addition, because water heats only to its boiling point, 212° F, poultry prepared this way will never burn—browning can only occur at higher temperatures—and can almost be ignored as it cooks. To maximize the transfer of heat from its source to liquid to food, the best cooking dishes for these methods are made from materials that are good heat conductors.

TENDERNESS IS THE GOAL

Cooking poultry in gently bubbling stock, broth, wine, or even plain water will tenderize even the toughest meat. Depending on the age of the bird, it will take anywhere from 30 minutes to 3 hours of complete or partial immersion in hot liquid to break down tough connective tissue and muscle to the point where the meat can be easily pierced with a fork. During this time the heat draws out flavor from the bird and whatever cooks with it into the cooking liquid.

Traditionally, *stewing hens*, 12- to 15-month-old birds past their usefulness as producers of eggs or chicks, simmered in the stew pot. Their well-exercised flesh takes the longest to tenderize, but gives up the most flavor. Quicker-to-cook younger chickens, such as fryers and roasters, as well as turkey, duck, goose, and some game birds—any poultry that can withstand long, slow cooking without falling apart—are now also used. The number of servings desired as well as the time available for preparation determine which bird to use.

While moist heat is easy to regulate and maintain, and is the best way to tenderize tough meat, the temperature at which poultry is cooked is critical to the quality of the final product. Poultry can still end up dry and tough even after hours in the stew pot if the cooking liquid was too hot. Keep it just below its boiling point, barely more than a simmer. At this temperature bubbles will rise lazily to the surface without the turbulence of a rolling boil. In the oven, an equivalent temperature would be 300° F to 325° F.

STEWING AND BRAISING: ALMOST BUT NOT QUITE THE SAME

Poultry stews and braises, including casseroles, ragouts, and daubes, are so similar technically that they are almost identical preparations. Both are cooked over low heat, in liquid in a covered pot, for an extended period of time. Both are easily prepared, economical, full of flavor, and hold well. They are wonderful do-ahead meals, tasting even better a day or so after cooking when the flavors have had a chance to blend, and they can be frozen without any loss of quality. However, despite all these similarities, stews and braises are more like fraternal than identical twins; braising calls for less liquid and the poultry is usually whole or in large pieces, whereas in a stew the meat is generally in small pieces.

Stews and braises offer considerable opportunity for the cook to be creative, as long as the ingredients have similar cooking times. Hardier root vegetables such as onions, carrots, and parsnips, prized for their sweet flavor, hold up well when cooked for a long time. More delicate additions that will lose their color and shape when overcooked, like mushrooms, potatoes, peas, and green beans, should be mixed in during the final 20 to 30 minutes. If the dish is made ahead, these vegetables can go into the pot during the reheating period.

BRAISING USES LESS LIQUID

Braising is a combination of cooking methods. Poultry pieces or whole birds are first sautéed in fat for color and extra flavor (or browned under

the broiler) and then slow-cooked in a relatively small amount of liquid until tender. The browned poultry is often set on a bed of chopped aromatic vegetables (*mirepoix*), which later may be puréed, mixed with the pan juices, and used as the sauce. About ¼ to ½ inch of liquid—water, stock, wine, hard cider, tomato purée—is added to the bottom of the pot, which is tightly covered to prevent evaporation. The liquid may need to be replenished during cooking if it cooks down too much. Cooking is completed either on top of the stove or in the oven.

Any casserole with a tight-fitting lid—a Dutch oven is usual—is suitable for braising. It's important that the vessel be of a material that conducts heat evenly and efficiently to prevent scorching and hot spots. The pot should not be much bigger than the fowl plus its liquid, so the heat will be directed to the meat rather than the empty spaces.

Brunswick Stew (see page 81) is an American creation named after Brunswick County, Virginia. Succotash, a main ingredient, was borrowed from the Indians by southern settlers, who incorporated it into their own cooking.

Rock Cornish game hens, small hybrids weighing about 1 to 1½ pounds each, are suited to a number of cooking methods. Here, they are prepared in the style of the poultry classic coq au vin, with onions and mushrooms in a red-wine sauce.

beurre manié (flour and butter kneaded together). Accompanying ingredients are like those used in a braise. The cooking pot is always tightly covered.

Fricassees are poultry stews with a white sauce. The poultry is sometimes lightly sautéed and the cooking liquid is most often white wine. After cooking the sauce is bound with a white roux and enriched with egg yolk and cream. Fricassees can also be made ahead, up to the point of adding the enrichment. The egg yolk and cream should be stirred in when the dish is reheated, as the sauce will separate if overcooked.

FINISHING, STORING, AND REHEATING

One of the most attractive features of stews and braises is that while they may take time to prepare, once done they keep well and need only to be reheated to serve. The cook should actually plan on making these dishes in advance as the flavors marry and improve with resting time. Stews and braises will keep up to one week in the refrigerator, and up to two months in the freezer.

No matter when the dish is to be served, immediately or later on, any fat should be skimmed away after cooking. This is most easily accomplished when the dish has cooled and the fat congealed on the surface. If it is to be refrigerated or frozen, cool it first at room temperature.

To reheat from the refrigerator, use a very low temperature to just warm the meat, avoiding further cooking. If raw vegetables are to be added at this point, increase the heat to medium-low and cook, covered, for 10 to 20 minutes, until the vegetables are tender and cooked through. To reheat from the freezer, first thaw the stew, then refrigerate until ready to reheat.

For browning, poultry should be dry and at room temperature, and the butter or oil properly heated. Crowding pieces into the pan will cause the meat to steam instead of brown (see pages 55–57 for a discussion of sautéing); if necessary, sauté only a few pieces at a time. All but a few tablespoons of the fat should be drained off before the remaining ingredients are added.

When the meat is tender when pierced, it's removed from the pan so that a sauce can be made with the pan juices. The sauce can be thickened by reducing the liquid, or by adding flour, cream, sour cream, or a vegetable purée (see page 104 for a more complete discussion of sauces and thickeners).

STEWS USE MORE LIQUID

Stews are usually made of small pieces of meat totally covered with liquid, most often water. The meat may or may not be browned first, and the cooking liquid becomes the sauce, which can be thickened with flour or

PERSIAN BRAISED CHICKEN

Onion slices sautéed until blackened add deep color and extra sweetness to this sauce. Its concentrated flavor is wonderful served over the braised chicken and an accompaniment of steamed rice.

> Salt
> 1 eggplant, sliced into half-moons ¼ inch thick
> 1 frying chicken (3 to 4 lbs), cut into serving pieces
> Freshly ground black pepper
> 1 cup oil
> 1 large onion, thinly sliced

1. Salt both sides of eggplant slices. Lay slices on paper towels and let rest for 1 hour to draw out excess moisture.

2. Wash chicken pieces and pat dry. Sprinkle lightly with salt and pepper.

3. In a Dutch oven over medium-high heat, heat 2 tablespoons of the oil. Add chicken and sauté until golden brown (about 7 minutes per side). Drain off fat. Remove pan from heat and set aside.

4. In a medium, heavy-bottomed skillet over medium-high heat, heat 3 tablespoons of the oil. Add onion slices and sauté until they are almost black (about 15 minutes). Remove onions from skillet and set aside.

5. Pat eggplant slices dry. In same skillet over medium-high heat, heat 3 tablespoons of the oil. Add a layer of eggplant slices and sauté until deep brown on both sides (about 5 minutes per side). Continue sautéing eggplant, one layer at a time, adding more oil as needed, until it is all browned.

6. In the Dutch oven, layer onion slices on top of chicken. Add enough water to reach halfway up chicken. Bring to a boil, reduce heat to medium-low, and simmer, covered, until chicken is tender when pierced with a fork (45 to 50 minutes). During last 15 minutes of simmering, add eggplant to heat through.

Serves 4.

GAME HENS "COQ AU VIN"

Classically, coq au vin uses a stewing hen. The tender game hens are a tasty alternative and speed the cooking time considerably.

> 2 Rock Cornish game hens (1 to 1½ lbs each), cut into serving pieces
> Salt and freshly ground black pepper
> ½ cup butter
> ¼ cup brandy
> Dry red wine (about 4 cups)
> Bouquet garni (3 sprigs parsley, 1 bay leaf, 1 teaspoon dried thyme, 1 teaspoon dried marjoram, wrapped in a 4-in. square of cheesecloth)
> 3 slices salt pork (each ½ in. thick)
> 12 small boiling onions, peeled
> 12 mushroom caps
> Beurre manié (3 tablespoons flour and 3 tablespoons butter kneaded together)

1. Wash game hens and pat dry; season with salt and pepper. In a large, heavy-bottomed sauté pan over medium-high heat, melt butter. Add game hens and sauté until golden brown (about 5 minutes per side). Drain fat from pan.

2. Pour brandy over game hens and flame it. When flame dies down, add enough red wine to cover hens. Add bouquet garni and cook, covered, over medium heat until game hens are tender when pierced with a fork (about 30 minutes).

3. After 15 minutes, in a medium, heavy-bottomed sauté pan over medium-high heat, brown salt pork. Add onions and sauté until a rich brown color (about 10 minutes). Add mushrooms and continue cooking until just tender (about 1 minute). Set aside.

4. When chicken is tender, remove bouquet garni. Add vegetables. Drop beurre manié into sauce and whisk to blend, cooking over medium heat until sauce has thickened.

Serves 4.

CHICKEN GUMBO

Gumbo is a Creole casserole that commonly uses okra as a thickener. Okra is best when purchased fresh in season during the summer months.

> 1 frying chicken (3 to 4 lbs), cut into serving pieces
> 4 slices bacon
> 1 pound smoked ham, cubed
> 1 medium onion, coarsely chopped
> 6 medium, ripe tomatoes, seeded and coarsely chopped, or 1 can (28 oz) Italian plum tomatoes, drained and coarsely chopped
> 4 cups sliced fresh okra or 2 packages (10 oz each) frozen okra
> 2 tablespoons crushed, dried, red pepper flakes
> Salt

1. Wash chicken pieces and pat dry. In a Dutch oven cook bacon over medium-high heat until well done (about 8 minutes). Remove bacon slices and set aside to cool. Leave bacon drippings in pan. When bacon is cool, crumble and reserve.

2. Add chicken and ham to hot bacon fat in Dutch oven and sauté over medium-high heat until golden brown (15 to 20 minutes).

3. Add crumbled bacon, onion, tomatoes, and okra. Cover and cook over medium heat for about 10 minutes. Add red pepper flakes, stirring to blend. Cover and cook another 15 to 20 minutes. Season with salt.

Serves 4 to 6.

BRAISED DUCK WITH BLACKBERRY-ORANGE SAUCE

This is an easy yet impressive dish, similar to duck à l'orange but with a refreshing addition of blackberry.

> 1 duckling (4 to 5 lbs)
> Salt and freshly ground black pepper
> 3 tablespoons oil
> Bouquet garni (3 sprigs parsley, 1 bay leaf, 1 teaspoon dried thyme, 1 teaspoon dried marjoram, wrapped in a 4-in. square of cheesecloth)

Blackberry-Orange Sauce

> ⅓ cup fresh orange juice
> ⅓ cup seedless blackberry jam
> 1 tablespoon white vinegar
> 2 teaspoons soy sauce
> 1 tablespoon cornstarch dissolved in 2 tablespoons water

1. Preheat oven to 325° F. Wash duck and pat dry; trim away excess fat. Season cavity with salt and pepper; truss. Prick skin several times with the point of a trussing needle or tip of a small knife. Salt and pepper outside of duck.

2. In a Dutch oven over medium-high heat, heat oil. Add duck, breast side down, and sauté until evenly browned (about 20 minutes). Drain off excess fat.

3. Position duck, breast side up, in Dutch oven. Add bouquet garni. Cover and set Dutch oven on middle rack of oven and roast until duck is tender (about 1 hour).

4. When duck is done, remove from Dutch oven and prepare Blackberry-Orange Sauce.

5. Remove string from duck, carve, and serve with sauce.

Serves 2 to 4.

Blackberry-Orange Sauce

Degrease pan drippings by spooning off excess fat. About ⅔ cup degreased drippings should remain. To the drippings, add orange juice, blackberry jam, vinegar, and soy sauce. Stir over medium-high heat until blended. Add cornstarch paste and stir until sauce has thickened.

Makes about ⅔ cup.

HONEY-BRAISED CHICKEN WITH DRIED FRUITS

Add the lemon slices just before serving. If allowed to cook too long, they will give the sauce a bitter taste.

> 1 frying chicken (3 to 4 lbs), cut into serving pieces
> Salt
> Ground allspice
> 3 tablespoons oil
> 2 shallots, thinly sliced
> ½ cup Chicken Stock (see page 91)
> ¼ cup honey
> 2 teaspoons grated fresh ginger
> ⅓ pound dried apricots
> 1 tablespoon raisins
> 1 lemon, thinly sliced

1. Wash chicken pieces and pat dry. Season with salt and allspice. In a Dutch oven, heat oil over medium-high heat. Add chicken and sauté until golden brown (about 7 minutes per side). Add shallots and sauté until golden brown (about 7 minutes).

2. In a small bowl mix stock, honey, and ginger. Add to chicken, stirring and scraping with a wooden spoon to loosen any browned bits that may have stuck to bottom of pan. Add apricots and raisins. Cook, covered, over medium-low heat until chicken is tender when pierced with a fork (35 to 40 minutes).

3. Add lemon slices and cook until heated through (about 3 minutes).

Serves 4 to 6.

POULET TANGIERS

This North African braise produces a zesty orange-ginger sauce sweetened with honey. Serve over steamed rice or couscous.

> 1 frying chicken (3 to 4 lbs), cut into serving pieces
> Salt and freshly ground black pepper
> 2 tablespoons oil
> 1 orange, quartered
> Juice of 1 orange
> 1 tablespoon grated fresh ginger
> 1 cup dry red wine
> ½ cup honey
> Grated rind of 1 orange
> 1 tablespoon cornstarch dissolved in 2 tablespoons water

1. Preheat oven to 325° F. Wash chicken pieces and pat dry. Season with salt and pepper.

2. In a Dutch oven over medium-high heat, heat oil. Sauté chicken in oil until golden brown on both sides (about 7 minutes per side). Drain off fat.

3. Add orange, orange juice, and fresh ginger. Bake, covered, on middle rack of oven until chicken is tender when pierced with a fork (about 1 hour).

4. When done, remove chicken from Dutch oven and set aside. Add wine, honey, and orange rind to pan juices (pan juices should measure 1 cup). Bring sauce to a boil over medium-high heat. Reduce heat and simmer until sauce is reduced to about 1⅓ cups. Add cornstarch paste and stir constantly until sauce has thickened (about 2 minutes). Pour sauce over chicken and serve.

Serves 4.

Seasoned duck will be sautéed for crispness, then braised to tender perfection. Luscious Blackberry-Orange Sauce provides the finishing touch.

CHICKEN FRICASSEE

A fricassee is best served immediately after cooking.

- *1 stewing hen (about 5 lbs), cut into serving pieces*
- *Salt and freshly ground black pepper*
- *Flour*
- *¼ cup butter*
- *2 medium carrots, peeled and coarsely chopped*
- *2 celery stalks, coarsely chopped*
- *1 medium onion, coarsely chopped*
- *4 cups Chicken Stock (see page 91)*
- *1 cup dry white wine*
- *Bouquet garni (3 sprigs parsley, 1 bay leaf, 1 teaspoon dried thyme, 1 teaspoon dried marjoram, wrapped in a 4-in. square of cheesecloth)*

Mushroom Cream Sauce

- *¼ cup each butter and flour*
- *2 cups whipping cream*
- *4 egg yolks*
- *¼ pound mushrooms, quartered*

1. Wash chicken pieces and pat dry. Season with salt and pepper and dust with flour. In a Dutch oven over medium heat, melt butter. Add chicken and quickly sauté until golden (about 5 minutes per side). Add carrots, celery, and onion and sauté 2 minutes more.

2. Pour Chicken Stock and wine over chicken and vegetables, stirring and scraping to loosen any browned bits that may have stuck to bottom of pan. Add bouquet garni. Bring to a boil over high heat, reduce heat to medium-low, and simmer, covered, until chicken is tender when pierced (about 2 hours).

3. Remove chicken; set aside. Strain stock, discarding vegetables and bouquet garni. Skim fat from surface; about 5 cups of stock should remain. Prepare Mushroom Cream Sauce.

4. Place chicken back in Dutch oven. Pour sauce over chicken and serve.

Serves 4 to 6.

Mushroom Cream Sauce In a medium, heavy-bottomed saucepan over medium heat, melt butter. Add flour, stirring to blend; cook 2 to 3 minutes. Pour in reserved stock, stirring constantly to blend. When sauce has thickened, remove from heat. In a bowl whisk cream with egg yolks. Pour some sauce into cream-yolk mixture, stirring to blend. Pour mixture into sauce, stirring constantly. Add mushrooms, return to heat, and heat through; do not boil.

Makes about 6 cups.

SPICY PEANUT CHICKEN

Like many Chinese dishes, this casserole is colorful and richly textured.

- *1 roasting chicken (4 to 5 lbs), cut into serving pieces*
- *¼ cup oil*
- *1 onion, thinly sliced*
- *1 cup Chicken Stock (see page 91)*
- *⅓ cup hoisin sauce*
- *¼ cup each soy sauce and pale dry sherry*
- *2 tablespoons rice wine vinegar*
- *1 teaspoon sugar*
- *3 cloves garlic, crushed*
- *1 slice fresh ginger*
- *1 package (1 oz) dried shiitake mushrooms, soaked according to package directions, drained, and quartered*
- *1 bunch broccoli, cut into florets*
- *⅓ cup roasted peanuts*
- *2 teaspoons dried, crushed, red pepper flakes*

1. Wash chicken pieces and pat dry. In a large, heavy-bottomed sauté pan over medium-high heat, heat oil. Add chicken and sauté until golden brown (about 7 minutes per side). Add onion and sauté until golden brown (about 4 minutes).

2. In a small bowl combine Chicken Stock, hoisin sauce, soy sauce, sherry, vinegar, and sugar. Pour over chicken, stirring and scraping to loosen any browned bits that may have stuck to bottom of pan. Add garlic and ginger; cook, covered, over medium-low heat 20 minutes.

3. Add mushrooms, broccoli, peanuts, and red pepper flakes. Cover; cook over medium-low heat until broccoli is tender (about 10 minutes). Serve.

Serves 4 to 6.

COUNTRY CAPTAIN

A classic chicken braise, Country Captain probably came to America from India via the British.

- *1 frying chicken (3 to 4 lbs), cut into serving pieces*
- *¾ cup flour*
- *1 teaspoon ground ginger*
- *1 teaspoon salt*
- *½ teaspoon freshly ground black pepper*
- *2 tablespoons butter*
- *2 tablespoons oil*
- *1 small onion, coarsely chopped*
- *1 clove garlic, crushed*
- *1 cup Chicken Stock (see page 91)*
- *2 teaspoons curry powder*
- *6 medium, ripe tomatoes, cored, seeded, and diced, or 1 can (14½ oz) Italian plum tomatoes, coarsely chopped, with juice*
- *3 tablespoons raisins or currants*

1. Wash chicken pieces and pat dry. Sift together flour, ginger, salt, and pepper. Dredge chicken in seasoned flour; shake off excess.

2. In a large, heavy-bottomed sauté pan over medium-high heat, heat butter and oil. Add chicken and sauté until golden brown (about 7 minutes per side). Set chicken aside.

3. In same pan sauté onion and garlic in remaining butter and oil over medium-high heat until translucent (about 4 minutes). Add Chicken Stock, stirring and scraping to loosen any browned bits that may have stuck to bottom of pan. Add curry powder and stir to blend.

4. Add tomatoes and cook until tender (about 1 minute). Correct seasonings.

5. Return chicken to pan, bring to a boil, and reduce heat to medium-low. Simmer, covered, until chicken is tender when pierced (about 30 minutes). Add raisins and serve.

Serves 4.

BRUNSWICK STEW

This famous southern stew mixes succotash with chicken and often another meat. Here, ham shanks and veal bones flavor the chicken stock.

> 1 pound ham shanks
> 1 pound veal bones
> 8 cups Chicken Stock (see page 91)
> 3 cups boneless, skinned chicken, cubed
> 4 medium, unpeeled russet potatoes, cubed
> 2 medium onions, coarsely chopped
> 2 cups fresh lima beans or 1 package (10 oz) frozen lima beans
> 2 cups fresh corn cut from the cob or 1 package (10 oz) frozen corn kernels
> 3 medium, ripe tomatoes, seeded and cubed or 1 can (14½ oz) Italian plum tomatoes, drained and chopped
> ¼ teaspoon crushed, dried, red pepper flakes
> Salt
> ½ cup pale dry sherry

1. In a Dutch oven, put ham shanks, veal bones, and chicken stock. If necessary, add water so that liquid covers bones. Bring slowly to a boil, partially covered, over medium heat. Reduce heat to medium-low and simmer for 1 hour. Skim off any scum as it rises to surface.

2. Strain stock; set bones aside to cool. Skim off fat. Remove meat from bones and reserve; discard bones.

3. Pour stock back into pot. Add meat from bones, chicken, potatoes, onions, lima beans, and corn. Bring to

a boil, reduce heat to medium-low, and simmer, covered, about 45 minutes. Add tomatoes, red pepper flakes, and salt. Simmer until stew has thickened (about 1 to 1½ hours), adding sherry for last 15 minutes.

Makes 12 cups.

GREEK CHICKEN STEW

Full of fresh vegetables, this cinnamon-spiced stew also features ripe Mediterranean olives.

> 1 frying chicken (3 to 4 lbs), cut into serving pieces
> ¼ cup extra-virgin olive oil
> 6 cloves garlic
> 2 medium onions, thinly sliced
> 2 cups Chicken Stock (see page 91)
> 1 cup dry red wine
> 1 can (6 oz) tomato paste
> 1 teaspoon ground cinnamon
> 4 small, red-skinned potatoes, cubed
> 3 medium carrots, peeled and coarsely chopped
> ½ pound fresh green beans, coarsely chopped
> 4 ounces Kalamata or other Mediterranean olives
> Salt and freshly ground black pepper

1. Wash chicken pieces and pat dry. In a Dutch oven over medium-high heat, heat oil. Add chicken pieces and sauté until golden brown (about 7 minutes per side). Add garlic and onions, cooking until soft and golden (about 10 minutes).

2. In a small bowl mix Chicken Stock, wine, tomato paste, and cinnamon. Pour over chicken, stirring and scraping to loosen any browned bits that may have stuck to bottom of pan. Simmer, covered, over medium-low heat until chicken is tender when pierced (about 25 minutes).

3. Add potatoes, carrots, and green beans. Cook, covered, over medium-low heat until vegetables are tender (about 20 minutes). Add olives. Season to taste and serve.

Serves 4 to 6.

THREE-MUSHROOM CHICKEN

Although costly, the wild mushrooms add a woodsy quality to this fricassee that the domestic variety can't match.

> 1 roasting chicken (4 to 5 lbs), cut into serving pieces
> ⅓ cup flour
> ⅓ ounce each dried porcini, morel, and oyster mushrooms
> 2 tablespoons each oil and butter
> 2 shallots, thinly sliced
> 1½ cups dry white wine
> ¾ cup Chicken Stock (see page 91)
> ½ cup whipping cream
> Salt and freshly ground black pepper

1. Wash chicken pieces and pat dry. Dredge in flour and shake off excess. In a small bowl combine mushrooms. Cover with water; soak 30 to 60 minutes.

2. In a large, heavy-bottomed skillet over medium-high heat, heat oil and butter. Add shallots and sauté until golden brown (about 3 minutes).

3. Add chicken to same skillet and sauté until golden brown (about 7 minutes per side).

4. Drain mushrooms, reserving water. In a small bowl combine ¾ cup of the mushroom water, the wine, and Chicken Stock. Add to skillet, stirring and scraping to loosen any browned bits that may have stuck to bottom of pan. Cook, covered, over medium-low heat until chicken is tender when pierced (20 to 25 minutes).

5. Squeeze all moisture from mushrooms; dice; add to chicken and stir to blend. Add whipping cream; stir to blend. Season with salt and pepper. Cover; cook gently over low heat to blend flavors, 3 to 5 minutes. Serve.

Serves 4 to 6.

menu

A TASTE OF HUNGARY

Poussin Paprikash

Noodles With Poppy Seeds

Creamed Peas

Beet Salad

Walnut-Apple Strudel

Imported Beer

Hungarian cooking is a lively blend of spicy and sweet. Poussin Paprikash is a paprika-spiced fricassee that substitutes quick-cooking young birds for the usual older and less tender chicken. Walnut-Apple Strudel is a typically Hungarian dessert. Note that the filo dough used as the pastry must be thawed in the refrigerator for eight hours.

POUSSIN PAPRIKASH

> 2 *poussins (1 lb each), halved*
> *Salt and freshly ground black pepper*
> 3 *tablespoons butter*
> 1 *tablespoon oil*
> 1 *large onion, thinly sliced*
> ⅓ *to ½ cup Chicken Stock (see page 91)*
> 1 *tablespoon sweet or hot Hungarian paprika*
> 1 *cup sour cream*
> 1 *tablespoon flour*

1. Wash poussins and pat dry. Season with salt and pepper; set aside.

2. In a medium, heavy-bottomed skillet over medium-high heat, heat butter and oil. Add poussins and sauté, starting skin side down, until golden brown (about 10 minutes per side).

3. Add onion and sauté until translucent. Add Chicken Stock and paprika, stirring and scraping with a wooden spoon to loosen any browned bits that may have stuck to bottom of pan. Cook, covered, for 15 to 20 minutes. Remove poussins to serving platter.

4. In a small bowl combine sour cream and flour. Blend into sauce, stirring until well blended (about 1 minute). Pour sauce over poussins and serve.

Serves 4.

NOODLES WITH POPPY SEEDS

> 8 *cups salted water*
> 4 *ounces dry fettuccine*
> 5 *tablespoons butter*
> ¼ *cup poppy seed*

1. In a 4-quart saucepan bring salted water to a rapid boil. Add fettuccine, reduce heat, and simmer, partially covered, until noodles are just tender (about 8 minutes); pour into colander to drain.

2. In the same saucepan melt butter over medium heat and sauté poppy seed for 1 minute. Add fettuccine; toss to coat with butter and poppy seed.

Serves 4 to 6.

CREAMED PEAS

> 2 *tablespoons butter*
> 1½ *pounds fresh peas, shelled (see Note)*
> ¼ *cup water*
> 1 *teaspoon sugar*
> ½ *cup whipping cream*

1. In a small saucepan melt butter over low heat. Add peas, water, and sugar. Cook, covered, until just tender (about 7 to 10 minutes).

2. Pour in cream and simmer, uncovered, until slightly thickened (about 3 to 5 minutes).

Serves 4.

Note One package (10 oz) frozen peas can be substituted for the fresh ones. To cook, put frozen block of peas with butter and sugar into small saucepan and cook, covered, until tender. Continue with step 2.

BEET SALAD

> 4 *whole beets, cooked, peeled, and julienned*
> 1 *tablespoon white wine vinegar*
> 1 *teaspoon prepared horseradish*
> ¼ *teaspoon sugar*
> 1 *head Bibb lettuce, washed, dried, and separated into leaves*

1. In a medium bowl combine julienned beets, vinegar, horseradish, and sugar. Toss beets to coat.

2. Cover and refrigerate for 2 hours to blend flavors. Serve beets on a bed of lettuce.

Serves 4 to 6.

WALNUT-APPLE STRUDEL

- ½ cup unsalted butter
- 1 cup fresh white bread crumbs
- ½ cup coarsely chopped walnuts
- 2 large baking apples, cored and coarsely chopped
- ¼ cup sugar
- ¼ cup raisins
- 1 teaspoon ground cinnamon
- 6 sheets filo dough, thawed in refrigerator for 8 hours

1. Preheat oven to 350° F. Butter a baking sheet.

2. In a small sauté pan over medium heat, melt ¼ cup of the butter. Add bread crumbs and sauté until golden brown (about 7 minutes); set aside.

3. In a medium bowl combine walnuts, apples, sugar, raisins, and cinnamon; toss to coat walnuts and apples thoroughly.

4. Melt remaining butter in a small saucepan; remove from heat. Spread a damp cloth over work area. Stack 2 sheets filo dough on cloth. Brush top sheet with melted butter. Repeat twice more, stacking 2 sheets of dough each time.

5. Spread sautéed bread crumbs on top sheet of dough, leaving a 3-inch border of dough uncovered all around. Cover bread crumbs with walnut-apple mixture.

6. With longer edge of dough facing you, fold nearest edge back over filling, then lift cloth and roll dough and filling like a jelly roll. Seal seam with water. Pinch edges to seal; tuck under.

7. Place on buttered baking sheet; brush top with melted butter. Set sheet on center rack of oven and bake until strudel is golden brown (about 25 to 35 minutes). Slice roll into individual servings about 1½ inches wide.

Serves 4 to 6.

Poussin Paprikash, served over Noodles With Poppy Seeds, is flanked by Creamed Peas and Walnut-Apple Strudel. In the foreground is Beet Salad. Paprika, a staple ingredient in Hungarian cuisine, is ground from sweet or hot red peppers or a combination of the two. Try to use imported Hungarian paprika for the Poussin Paprikash; it is considered the best in quality and will improve both the flavor and the color of the dish. Like all stews, this one can be made up to a week in advance and held in the refrigerator, or frozen for up to two months. Gentle reheating is essential or the sauce will separate.

Poule au Pot is a complete meal in itself. Vegetables and a rich stuffing—composed of ground beef and pork, onion, bread crumbs, cream, and seasonings—cook as a whole chicken poaches.

POACHING: GENTLE AND JUICY

When the cook wants an especially delicate poultry flavor, poaching is ideal. Whole birds or breasts are immersed in a clear liquid—water or plain stock—and gently simmered (never boiled), just until the meat is tender and succulently moist—overcooking will cause the meat to be tough and dry. Boneless breasts finish quickly, taking only 6 to 7 minutes. Whole chickens will cook in anywhere from 25 minutes to 2 to 3 hours, depending on their size and age. Poached poultry is perfect when cooked meat is needed for salads and sandwiches, or when a light, plain flavor is desired, without the color or

fatty taste developed in sautéing. And the cooking liquid becomes a flavorful stock ready to be served as a first course or used in another recipe.

POACHED CHICKEN BREASTS WITH RED WINE VINEGAR

Gentle poaching produces mildly flavored chicken breasts, which are then bathed in a tangy sauce of crème fraîche enlivened with shallots and wine vinegar.

> 1 cup Chicken Stock (see page 91)
> 2 whole chicken breasts, halved, boned, and skinned
> ⅓ cup red wine vinegar
> 2 tablespoons minced shallots
> ¾ cup butter, cut in small pieces
> 3 tablespoons Crème Fraîche (see page 108)

1. In a small sauté pan over medium heat, bring Chicken Stock to a gentle boil. Slip in chicken breast halves, reduce heat to medium-low, and simmer, partially covered, until chicken is tender when pierced with a fork (about 10 minutes). Remove chicken and set aside.

2. In a small saucepan over medium-high heat, bring vinegar and shallots to a boil. Reduce heat to medium-low and simmer until vinegar has been reduced to about 2 tablespoons (7 to 10 minutes).

3. Add butter, a piece at a time, stirring constantly. Allow each piece of butter to melt and be incorporated into sauce before adding next piece. Sauce will gradually thicken.

4. Turn off heat and whisk in Crème Fraîche. Serve sauce over poached breasts.

Serves 4.

POULE AU POT

Poule au pot is the traditional Sunday supper in France. This stuffed, poached chicken produces a rich broth that can be served as a first course or saved for later use.

⅓ pound ground beef
1 egg white
⅓ cup half-and-half
3 tablespoons butter
½ cup dry bread crumbs
½ pound ground pork
One fourth of a medium onion, finely chopped
1 clove garlic, minced
½ teaspoon dried thyme
1 frying chicken (3 to 4 lbs)
16 cups Chicken Stock (see page 91) or water
Bouquet garni (3 sprigs parsley, 1 bay leaf, 1 teaspoon dried thyme, 1 teaspoon dried marjoram, wrapped in a 4-in. square of cheesecloth)
Salt and freshly ground black pepper
3 small carrots, peeled and cut in 4-inch pieces
3 ribs celery, cut in 4-inch pieces
2 parsnips, peeled and cut in 4-inch pieces

1. In medium bowl of electric mixer or in food processor, combine the ground beef and egg white. Slowly pour in half-and-half, beating or processing continuously. Set aside.

2. In a small saucepan over medium heat, melt butter. Add bread crumbs and sauté until golden brown.

3. In another medium bowl, using hands, combine ground pork, onion, garlic, and thyme. Mix in bread crumbs. Add ground beef mixture and mix in with hands.

4. Wash chicken. Remove innards and trim away excess fat. Stuff cavity with meat mixture. Sew up vent with trussing needle and string. Truss chicken and wrap loosely with cheesecloth.

5. Place chicken in Dutch oven and cover with Chicken Stock. Bring slowly to a boil and skim off any scum from the surface of the cooking liquid. Add bouquet garni and lightly season with salt and pepper. Simmer, covered, over medium-low heat until chicken is tender when pierced with a fork (about 1½ hours). During the last 30 minutes of cooking, add carrots, celery, and parsnips; simmer until tender.

6. When chicken and vegetables are tender, remove chicken to a carving board. Remove cheesecloth, then stuffing, and carve chicken. Remove vegetables from Dutch oven with slotted spoon onto a serving platter. Arrange carved chicken with vegetables and stuffing on the platter and serve.

Serves 4.

PERFECTLY POACHED CHICKEN FOR SALADS AND SANDWICHES

1 chicken (fryer, roaster, capon, or stewing hen)
2 medium carrots and 2 ribs celery, both coarsely chopped
1 large onion, quartered
Bouquet garni (3 sprigs parsley, 1 bay leaf, 1 teaspoon dried thyme, 1 teaspoon dried marjoram, wrapped in a 4-in. square of cheesecloth)

1. Wash chicken, remove innards, and trim away excess fat. Place in a stockpot or Dutch oven with carrots, celery, onion, and bouquet garni. Add enough cold water to cover.

2. Bring slowly to a boil, partially covered. Skim. Reduce heat to medium-low and simmer gently, covered, until bird is just tender when pierced (see "Timetable for Poaching Chicken," at left).

3. Remove bird from pot and set aside to cool. Strain broth and save for another use. When chicken is cool, remove meat from bones.

Makes 3 to 5 cups, depending on which bird is used.

Homemade stock adds flavor to sauces and soups. Here, Chicken Stock (see page 91) enriches Cream of Curry Chicken Soup (see page 94).

Stocks, Soups & Sauces

Stocks, soups, and sauces are among the great basic foods. Stocks, developed from meat, bones, and vegetables slowly cooked in liquid, provide a base of flavor upon which a recipe can be built. Soups are sustaining, appetite-piquing, comforting. Sauces are the glory of classic French cuisine, and ideal partners for poultry. In this chapter, you'll find a generous selection of stock and soup recipes and garnishes (see pages 91–97) plus a soup-party menu, and a multitude of sauces, including flavored butters for lighter toppings (see pages 102–109).

STARTING POINTS FOR FINE COOKING

Soups are comfort foods that nourish the spirit as well as the body. The restorative powers of soup have been described in literature for hundreds of years. In the twelfth century, philosopher-physician Moses Maimonides praised chicken soup as an "excellent food and medication," and prescribed the meat and broth of hens and roosters as a cure for some diseases. Today, soups and sauces prepared from scratch with the freshest ingredients communicate care, an investment of extra effort at a time when so much of what we eat comes from cans and boxes.

Making stock, the basis of good soups and sauces, is itself a gentle, slow, and soothing process. Flavor and nutrients are gradually extracted from meat, bones, and vegetables into the surrounding liquid. The concentrated brew that is the end product of this process is considered the backbone of cooking, the essence of fine flavor.

At times, the divisions between stock, soup, or sauce are so finely drawn they are almost nonexistent. A strained stock, the common antecedent of both soups and sauces, becomes bouillon simply by being put in a bowl and served at the table. Although soup is a meal in itself, or one course of a meal, and a sauce is always an accompaniment, never eaten by itself, some soups are in composition no more than thin sauces. What is most important to remember when trying to sort stocks, soups, and sauces into some logical culinary hierarchy is that stocks come first. However they are seasoned, extended, thickened, or garnished, in their original state, stocks are the building blocks of cooking.

STOCKS: A FOUNDATION OF FLAVOR

To the French, stocks are the foundation of all cuisine. Their purpose is to provide a base of flavor upon which a recipe can be built. These rich brews develop from slow-cooking meat, bones, and vegetables in liquid to extract their nutrients and flavor and to draw out other natural materials that add desirable body and texture. Stock is the starting point, or critical ingredient, of a multitude of dishes, particularly soups and sauces. Early in this century, master chef Auguste Escoffier wrote that it is the quality of the stock that determines the success of the final product. Even supremely talented cooks, Escoffier asserted, can do no better than the ingredients with which they work. Some sixty years before Escoffier expounded this view, the popular British cookbook author Mrs. Beeton instructed all of Victorian England that "it is on a good stock that excellence in cookery depends."

Poultry stocks are perhaps the most versatile, and the most familiar of all stocks. Their mild yet distinctive flavor allows them to be paired with a cornucopia of ingredients. They play an important role in most of the world's cuisines.

Most likely our grandmothers had stockpots simmering on the stove a good deal of the time. Into the gently cooking liquid were added poultry carcasses, scraps of skin and meat, leftover bones, and fresh vegetables and herbs, which slowly released their flavorful essences to produce a rich and nourishing broth. Today's cook more often uses a prepared stock or broth. However, a taste comparison of two soups, one prepared with a homemade stock and the other with water or canned broth or bouillon, will impel you to get out the stockpot: The difference in taste is striking.

A supply of stock, stored in serving-sized portions in your freezer, will actually simplify meal preparation, as well as improve its presentation. A sautéed chicken breast, quickly cooked, becomes luxurious when finished with a wonderful blend of pan juices, some stock, and seasonings, put together just before serving. A hearty vegetable soup is no all-day affair when the broth has already been made: Combine the liquid base with chunks of fresh vegetables and cooked chicken, and perhaps some whimsically shaped dried pasta, then cook just until the additions are tender and the meat reheated.

In cooking, as with most challenging endeavors, flexibility is essential. Lack of a quality stock will not ruin a meal, just as using your own stock will not guarantee its success. Fine sauces and soups *can* be prepared with commercial bases. Homemade stocks, however, do add a special dimension to cooking. Stock-making needn't be a weekly ritual, but it is a procedure with which all good cooks should be comfortably familiar.

Which Stock to Use?

The choice of which poultry stock the cook will choose for any particular purpose is mostly a matter of flavor. Generally, a stock will match the dish it is used to prepare. For example, for soups, chicken stock is the common choice. But no matter what the dish, the final decision is literally a matter of personal taste.

ABOUT POULTRY STOCK

A stock of good quality is the offspring of an arranged marriage between meat and bone, used for their flavor and thickening properties, and mildly flavored vegetables, incorpo-

rated for their sweetness and aroma. Water is the medium that brings these elements together. Unlike cooking with dry heat, where the goal is to retain precious juices, the process of extraction draws out flavor and nutrients from the stock ingredients into the simmering liquid. Also unlike roasting or grilling, it is not necessary to use only young, tender fowl for stock-making. When slowly cooked in moist heat, older birds actually release more flavor.

Traditionally the stockpot was the catchall for leftovers and less desirable raw poultry parts such as necks or feet. Scraps of meat, skin, and uncooked or cooked bones (what is left after boning a whole bird or any of its parts, or the carcass of a roasted bird) were saved for making

stock. Today's household does not habitually accumulate these basic stock ingredients, choosing instead to discard the seemingly unusable remains of the family's meals. However, cooks interested in trying their hand at stock-making should freeze leftovers for the stockpot until a sufficient amount has been collected.

Learning to prepare poultry stocks is an excellent introduction to the art of stock-making in general. The appeal of these stocks is their relatively quick cooking time—2 hours versus 8 to 12 for other meat stocks.

INGREDIENTS AND EQUIPMENT

In addition to the flesh, skin, and bones of fowl, poultry stock is made with aromatic vegetables, typically carrots, onions, celery, and often parsnips. Not unexpectedly, these are the components of *mirepoix*, the

Heat some homemade Chicken Stock (see page 91), add water chestnuts (either fresh or canned), sliced green onions, and cooked rice, and Chicken-Rice Soup (see page 93) is ready to serve.

STOCK IN ALL ITS GUISES

Although the terms stock, broth, bouillon, *and* consommé *are often used interchangeably, both in their preparation and in describing soup- and sauce-making, there are slight distinctions among them that are helpful to understand.*

Stock *is a liquid with a concentrated flavor derived from pieces of raw and cooked poultry, both bones and meat, plus vegetables that are slowly cooked until all the nutrients and flavor have been drawn into the cooking liquid. The additions are discarded—they have cooked beyond the point of edibility, both in consistency and taste. The liquid is strained, the fat skimmed away, and what remains is used to make soups and sauces.*

Broth *is the liquid left in the pot after pieces of raw poultry have been cooked just until done. The poultry and other ingredients that have cooked along with it are usually eaten, rather than discarded. Because broth is the by-product of a process designed to cook food so that it will still retain its shape and most of its flavor, broth cooks for a shorter time than stock. It is lighter than stock, and less richly flavored.*

Bouillon *is simply strained stock or broth. It is often served as a clear, garnished soup.*

Consommé *is bouillon that has been clarified. It becomes an elegant, flavorful soup, with an exceptionally pleasing clarity and depth of color.*

coarsely chopped vegetables placed in a roasting pan with the bird to improve the pan juices (see page 20). Avoid vegetables with strong flavors, such as cabbage or turnips, that would overpower other ingredients, and starchy vegetables, like potatoes, that would cloud the stock. Seasoning—salt, pepper, herbs—is meted out with a light hand since the reduction involved in making soups and sauces from stocks intensifies flavor and can turn seasoning into overseasoning. A *bouquet garni*, usually sprigs of fresh parsley, a bay leaf, some thyme, and some marjoram secured in a square of cheesecloth, is often all the seasoning necessary. If some salting is in order, wait until the last 15 minutes of cooking time.

Although not a difficult process, making stock *is* time-consuming, so it's most practical to prepare a large quantity at any one session—some to use right away and the rest to freeze. Use a large, heavy-bottomed stockpot, with at least an 8-quart capacity, or a Dutch oven. Also helpful, but not necessary, is a *chinois*, a conical sieve with a very fine mesh (see page 11) used to strain cooked stock. You can substitute a colander lined with several thicknesses of finely woven, dampened cheesecloth for a chinois, but do not use cloth with a loose weave. Stock is best frozen in plastic containers sized to match the amount needed for frequently prepared recipes.

COOKING THE STOCK

After the poultry and vegetables are in the pot, they are covered with *cold* water, more effective for drawing out flavorful essences than hot. The liquid is slowly brought to a boil, and then simmered for the remainder of the cooking time. The slow simmering, as opposed to a continuous boil, allows fat and albuminous material to rise to the surface, where it can be skimmed off at regular intervals. The skimming is important to obtaining a refined stock.

Toward the end of the cooking period, taste the stock. When its flavor is satisfactory, remove the pot from the heat and cool slightly. Although stock is meant to be cooked until all of the essences have been drawn out of the ingredients, leaving the additions limp and shapeless, it's important not to overcook it. Overcooking poultry stock will cause the delicate poultry bones to disintegrate, and the stock will be cloudy and full of bone marrow.

After the stock has cooled for a few minutes, remove bones and any solid material that can be easily captured with a wire skimmer or slotted spoon. Pour the liquid through a fine-mesh strainer or colander lined with tightly woven cheesecloth (or a tightly woven flour cloth) that has been rinsed and wrung almost dry. Cool completely.

Storing Cooked Stock

When stock has reached room temperature, cover and refrigerate. Chilling will congeal any fat, which can then be lifted off the surface of the liquid. However, if you are not planning to use the stock right away, let the layer of congealed fat sit on the chilled liquid since it acts as a shield, protecting the stock from bacterial contamination. Refrigerated stock will spoil if not used within three to five days. To extend its usability to a week to two weeks, boil refrigerated stock every two or three days.

Stock can be frozen for up to two months. You can put it in portion-sized containers—2-cup for sauce-making, larger for soups—or freeze it in ice cube trays, then transfer the cubes to plastic storage bags for easy access. Always boil refrigerated or frozen stock before using.

CLARIFYING STOCK

Some translucent sauces and some soups, such as consommé, require a clear liquid base, achieved by clarifying with egg whites and eggshells. As the whites coagulate in the hot liquid, they rise to the surface, trapping materials floating in the liquid.

To clarify, first completely degrease the broth by refrigerating until the fat hardens; remove the fat. It is critical that the liquid be grease-free as fat will interfere with the egg white's "trapping" ability. For 4 cups of stock, add 1 lightly beaten egg white and 1 eggshell. Simmer stock slowly for 10 minutes and remove from the heat. Skim off any scum that has risen to the surface, and strain by gently ladling stock through a colander lined with dampened cheesecloth or flour cloth.

When Homemade Stock Is Not Available

If the choice is between using a canned stock or not cooking, even culinary purists will opt for the commercial preparation, either by itself or to extend a too-small amount of their own stock. Canned broth or bouillon, although it has a slightly "tinny" taste, is an acceptable stock substitute if doctored somewhat. Do not use canned consommé in a recipe that calls for stock; it will be too sweet. Bouillon cubes are very salty, so use with care.

To bolster canned stock or broth: Mix 2 cups of canned stock with a small amount of finely chopped onion, celery, and carrots, plus 2 sprigs fresh parsley, half a bay leaf, and a pinch of thyme. Simmer 25 minutes; strain.

Basics

POULTRY STOCK

The process for stock-making is the same regardless of which bird is the main ingredient. Chicken and turkey are most commonly used to make stock, but other fowl may be used. Use whatever parts are available—carcass, cooked scraps, wing tips, giblets (excluding livers), skin, any leftovers—hoarded in the freezer.

CHICKEN, TURKEY, OR PHEASANT STOCK

> 2 or 3 chicken carcasses, or
> 1 turkey carcass, or
> 2 pheasant carcasses
> 2 carrots, peeled and cut
> in 4-inch slices
> 2 ribs celery, including tops,
> cut in 4-inch slices
> 1 onion, quartered
> 1 parsnip, peeled and cut
> in 4-inch slices

Bouquet garni (3 sprigs parsley, 1 bay leaf, 1 teaspoon dried thyme, 1 teaspoon dried marjoram, wrapped in a 4-in. square of cheesecloth)

1. Put carcasses in an 8-quart stockpot or Dutch oven. Add vegetables and bouquet garni. Add enough cold water to cover.

2. Bring to a boil, reduce heat to medium-low, and simmer, uncovered, for about 30 minutes; skim.

3. Simmer, partially covered, about 2 hours, skimming occasionally.

4. Remove carcasses and other bones and discard. Strain stock through a colander lined with several thicknesses of dampened cheesecloth. Cool, uncovered, at room temperature.

5. Refrigerate until fat rises to the surface and congeals (about 8 hours). If stock will be used within 3 to 5 days, leave fat; skim when ready to use. If stock is to be frozen, skim fat.

Makes 8 cups.

Consommé, like this one prepared from pheasant stock, has long been a popular and elegant first course for a formal meal.

SOUPS: SIMPLE, SATISFYING, SUPERB

Soup has a thousand faces. It can be part of a meal, or the meal itself. It can be as plain as the unadorned, soothing chicken broth we all sip as a tonic when we are ill, and as sophisticated and stylish as a sparkling pheasant consommé or a delicate cream of curry soup that might begin an elaborate, multicourse dinner. In between are the myriad combinations, textures, and consistencies that make soup cookery a delightful adventure for the creative cook, and soup everyone's favorite food. Poultry-based soups are particularly appealing. Easy to digest, they have a mild, universally appreciated flavor that marries well with a wide variety of other ingredients. If a stock is already available, soup is extremely easy and quick to prepare, ready for the table in less than 20 minutes.

In deciding how much soup to prepare, plan on ¾ cup for an appetizer serving and 1 cup for a main-dish serving.

A Liquid Food

Basically, soup is a liquid that has been cooked with additions intended to impart enough flavor and nutrients so that the final product becomes an appealing food. In cooking, soups are categorized as clear (broths, consommés), or thickened (cream soups, vegetable purées), light (consommés, bouillon, light cream soups) or hearty (dense vegetable soups and thick cream soups). Thickened soups develop their body almost identically to sauces. Thickeners include starches such as flour, cornstarch, or tapioca; cream; enrichments added with cream, such as egg yolk; puréed vegetables; or combinations of these ingredients. Soups also use rice and grains to impart bulk without actually thickening the liquid. (See page 104 for a more complete discussion of thickening agents.)

Finishing Touches

Whether you are serving a clear, pristine consommé, or a chunky chicken and vegetable combination, a garnish is always an appropriate finish. Garnishes impart imaginative touches of color, flavor, and texture that enhance the appeal of any dish. A sprinkling of chopped fresh parsley or, more exotically, a few strategically placed edible blossoms will delight the eye. When deciding what to use for a garnish, aim for a balance of color, texture, shape, and taste, and remember that garnishes are usually savory, not sweet. They can be a significant addition, such as dumplings, or a barely perceptible taste, like a paper-thin lemon slice floated on top of a soup. Poultry is so neutral in both flavor and color that a garnish for poultry-based soups is almost mandatory. And even thick and colorful soups are enhanced when a topping is added. See pages 96–97 for a selection of garnish recipes.

PHEASANT CONSOMMÉ

This is a light, garnished soup. Its appeal is in its sparkling clarity and depth of color and flavor.

- *3 cups salted water*
- *1 cup julienned leeks, carrots, and celery*
- *4 cups Pheasant Stock, strained and clarified (see page 91) Salt, if necessary*

1. In a 1-quart saucepan bring the water to a boil. Blanch the vegetables by cooking them in the boiling water for 1 minute; drain vegetables and set them aside.

2. In a medium saucepan over low heat, heat stock. Add blanched vegetables and salt, if necessary. Serve.

Makes 4 cups.

HUNTER'S CONSOMMÉ

The French have literally hundreds of recipes for consommés and other soups. Tapioca is the unusual but traditional thickener for this one.

- *2 cups duck consommé*
- *2 tablespoons quick-cooking tapioca*
- *⅓ cup Marsala wine*
- *¼ cup thinly sliced mushrooms Salt and freshly ground black pepper*
- *1 tablespoon minced parsley*

1. In a 4-quart saucepan over medium heat, bring consommé to a gentle boil. Add tapioca, reduce heat to medium-low, and simmer until tapioca is cooked (5 to 7 minutes).

2. Strain consommé through a colander lined with several thicknesses of dampened cheesecloth. Return strained consommé to pot.

3. Add Marsala and mushrooms, and heat through (about 2 minutes). Season with salt and pepper to taste. Garnish with parsley.

Makes about 2½ cups.

CHICKEN-RICE SOUP

This tasty soup is one delicious example of the practicality of having a supply of frozen homemade stock. With just a few additions, you have a flavorful, satisfying dish.

- *4 cups Chicken Stock (see page 91) or broth*
- *6 water chestnuts, thinly sliced*
- *2 green onions, thinly sliced (including green portion)*
- *1 cup cooked white rice Salt and white pepper*

1. In a medium saucepan over medium heat, bring stock to a gentle boil. Add water chestnuts and green onions. Reduce heat to medium-low and simmer until cooked through (about 7 minutes).

2. Add rice and heat through. Season with salt and pepper.

Makes 4 cups.

MEXICAN POZOLE

This recipe is a streamlined adaptation of a Mexican classic that usually uses pig's feet and pork.

    6 cups Chicken Stock (see
       page 91)
    1 onion, finely chopped
    1 clove garlic, minced
    1 can (29 oz) hominy, drained
    1 cup cubed raw chicken
       Salt and freshly ground
       black pepper
       Garnishes: 1 cup sliced radishes; 1 to 2 avocados, sliced in thin wedges; 2 limes, cut in wedges; 1 cup shredded lettuce

1. In a 4-quart saucepan bring stock to a boil. Add onion and garlic; reduce heat to medium-low and simmer until onion and garlic are soft (about 7 minutes).

2. Add hominy and heat through. Add chicken pieces and simmer until just tender (about 7 minutes). Season with salt and pepper.

3. Serve accompanied by garnishes set out in small bowls. Have guests garnish their own soup.

Makes 8 cups.

CREAM OF CURRY CHICKEN SOUP

An example of how fuzzy the line dividing soup and sauce can be, this velvety, curry-spiced soup is actually a thinned and seasoned béchamel sauce.

    ¼ cup butter
    ¼ cup flour
    2 cups half-and-half
    2 cups Chicken Stock (see
       page 91)
    2 teaspoons curry powder
    ¼ teaspoon salt
    ¼ teaspoon white pepper
    2 cups diced cooked chicken
    1 lemon, sliced paper-thin,
       for garnish

1. In a medium saucepan over medium heat, melt butter. Whisk in flour and cook just until golden.

2. Reduce heat and pour in half-and-half and Chicken Stock, whisking constantly until texture is smooth and velvety. Add curry powder, salt, and pepper. Adjust seasonings if necessary.

3. Add diced chicken; heat through. Garnish with thin slices of lemon.

Makes 4 cups.

HEARTY CHICKEN-VEGETABLE SOUP

This soup is designed to utilize ingredients on hand and can be modified to include whatever is available to you. Cooking time is only as long as it takes to tenderize the vegetables and pasta.

    6 cups Chicken Stock (see
       page 91)
    1 carrot, cut in ⅛-inch slices
    1 onion, cut in ¼-inch cubes
    1 cup dried small pasta
    1 small zucchini, cut in
       ¼-inch cubes
    1 large tomato, cut in
       ¼-inch cubes
    1½ cups cooked chicken, cut in
       ¼-inch cubes
    ½ cup minced parsley
    2 tablespoons tomato paste
       Salt and freshly ground
       black pepper

1. In a 4-quart saucepan over medium-high heat, bring stock to a gentle boil. Add carrot, onion, and pasta. Cover, reduce heat to medium-low, and simmer until vegetables and pasta are just tender (about 10 minutes).

2. Add zucchini, tomato, and chicken. Cover and cook until tender (about 5 minutes).

3. Add parsley and tomato paste. Stir to blend well. Season with salt and pepper.

Makes 6 cups.

CHICKEN SOUP WITH DUMPLINGS

Resist the urge to lift the lid when the dumplings are steaming and you will be rewarded with a light and tender product. When the lid is raised, steam escapes and the cooking temperature is lowered. In the time it takes to raise the temperature again, the dumplings will overcook.

    2 cups cake flour
    4 teaspoons baking powder
    1 teaspoon salt
    2 eggs, lightly beaten
    ¾ cup milk
   16 cups Chicken Stock (see
       page 91)
    6 small carrots, diced
    6 ribs celery, diced
    3 onions, finely chopped

1. In a large bowl sift together flour, baking powder, and salt. In a small bowl combine eggs and milk. Make a well in center of flour; pour egg-milk mixture into well and stir until well combined. Set aside.

2. In an 8-quart stockpot or Dutch oven, bring stock to a boil. Add carrots, celery, and onions; reduce heat to medium-low and simmer 10 minutes.

3. Drop dumpling batter into simmering broth, 1 tablespoon at a time. Cover and simmer for 10 minutes without lifting lid. Serve at once.

Makes 16 cups.

POTATO-LEEK SOUP

This soup derives its body from puréed vegetables. Chicken stock and cream are added to thin the purée.

> 4 medium leeks (white portion
>   only), roots trimmed
> 2 tablespoons butter
> 4 medium russet potatoes, peeled
>   and cut in ½-inch cubes
> 6 cups Chicken Stock (see
>   page 91)
> 2 cups whipping cream
>   Salt and white pepper

1. Wash leeks thoroughly to remove any dirt. Drain well, pat dry, and chop coarsely.

2. In a large, heavy-bottomed skillet over medium heat, melt butter. Add leeks and sauté until translucent. Reduce heat to medium-low, add cubed potatoes, and cook until nearly tender (about 15 minutes).

3. Pour in Chicken Stock and simmer, covered, over medium-low heat, until potatoes are fully tender (about 20 minutes). Remove from heat; cool.

4. Purée mixture in a food mill, blender, or food processor. Pour back into skillet, add cream, and heat through. Season with salt and pepper.

Makes 8 cups.

Keep homemade Chicken Stock (see page 91) on hand to be the base of an easily made ingredient-packed soup. Hearty Chicken-Vegetable Soup features fresh vegetables, pasta, and cubes of cooked chicken, quickly simmered into a filling meal-in-a-bowl.

Spinach and Parmesan cheese enliven creamy Gnocchi Verdi, flavorful dumplings that will enhance any clear soup, like the consommé shown here.

SOUP GARNISHES

Garnishes can be quite simple—a few spoonfuls of chopped fresh herbs or some vegetable slivers. They can also be quite elaborate and time-consuming, like delicate quenelles. Some garnishes work better for certain styles of soup than do others. Use the following lists as a guide, but certainly experiment on your own. Recipes for starred garnishes appear on the opposite page.

To make the best croutons, use a high-quality, dense bread, not an airy commercial loaf. When making dumplings, use low-protein cake flour for a lighter final product. Do not lift the lid from the pot while the dumplings steam or they will toughen. The batter for gnocchi can be prepared a

day ahead and refrigerated until needed. Your butcher can grind the chicken needed for the quenelles, or you can grind it at home with a food processor according to the manufacturer's instructions.

For Thick Soups

> *Croutons**
> *Grated cheese (try Parmesan or Romano)*
> *Julienned poultry, ham, or sausage*

For Cream Soups

> *Chopped nuts (particularly toasted slivered almonds)*
> *Dollop of sour cream or Crème Fraîche (page 108)*

For Clear Soups

> *Julienned vegetables (for consommé)*
> *Dumplings**
> *Gnocchi**
> *Quenelles**

For All Soups

Snipped fresh chives
Thin slices of lemon
Leeks cut in rings
Fluted mushroom caps
Thin slices of mushroom
Nasturtium blossoms
Fresh parsley sprigs or
chopped fresh parsley
Watercress leaves

CROUTONS

¼ cup butter
1 clove garlic, crushed
3 cups bread cubes (cut from
fresh bread in ¼-in. cubes)

1. In a medium, heavy-bottomed skillet over medium heat, melt butter. Add garlic. Reduce heat to medium-low and sauté until garlic has browned.

2. Add bread cubes and sauté over low heat until crisp and golden brown (10 to 15 minutes). Drain on paper towels.

Makes 3 cups.

GNOCCHI VERDI

1 pound fresh spinach (leaves
only), washed thoroughly
¼ cup butter
¾ cup cream cheese
2 eggs, lightly beaten
2 tablespoons whipping cream
½ cup freshly grated Parmesan
cheese
¼ cup flour
Salt and freshly ground
black pepper

1. Put moist spinach leaves into a large sauté pan. Cover and cook, without adding extra water, until spinach is limp (about 5 minutes).

2. Drain spinach thoroughly, pressing out any excess liquid; chop finely.

3. In the same skillet over medium heat, melt butter. Add spinach and cook until all moisture is evaporated (2 to 3 minutes).

4. Add cream cheese and cook, stirring constantly, to blend (about 5 minutes). Remove from heat and set aside.

5. In a small bowl combine eggs, cream, Parmesan cheese, and flour. Fold into spinach mixture in pan. Season with salt and pepper.

6. Pour gnocchi batter into a shallow dish and spread into a thin layer. Cover and refrigerate until firm (at least 2 hours).

7. When ready to cook, shape batter into walnut-sized balls; set aside.

8. Bring a 4-quart pot of salted water to a boil. Drop balls into water, reduce heat to medium-low, and simmer until they puff and rise to the surface. Remove with a slotted spoon and drain. Repeat until all batter has been used.

Makes 25 gnocchi.

CHICKEN QUENELLES

½ cup water
½ teaspoon salt
2 tablespoons butter
⅓ cup flour
1 egg
1 egg white
1 cup ground chicken
2 tablespoons whipping cream
2 tablespoons fresh watercress
leaves
Salt and white pepper
2 cups Chicken Stock (see
page 91)

1. In a 2-quart, heavy-bottomed saucepan, combine water, salt, and butter; simmer over medium-low heat until butter melts. Remove from heat.

2. With a wooden spoon, beat flour into butter liquid all at once. Cook over medium-high heat, beating continuously until mixture forms a ball and does not stick to sides of the pan. Remove from heat.

3. Beat in egg, then egg white; cool completely.

4. In a medium bowl combine chicken with cream, watercress, salt, and pepper. When flour mixture has completely cooled, combine with ground chicken mixture.

5. In a large, heavy-bottomed sauté pan or skillet over medium-low heat, simmer stock. Drop in quenelle batter, 1 tablespoon at a time, until pan is full. Simmer until quenelles puff and roll over easily (about 10 minutes). Remove with a slotted spoon. Repeat until all batter has been used.

Makes 20 quenelles.

DUMPLINGS

1 cup cake flour
2 teaspoons baking powder
½ teaspoon salt
1 egg, lightly beaten
⅓ to ½ cup milk

1. In a medium bowl sift together flour, baking powder, and salt. In a small bowl combine egg and ⅓ cup milk.

2. Make a well in center of flour. Pour liquid into well and stir to blend liquid and flour. Add more milk if necessary, but keep the batter stiff.

3. Bring a 3-quart pot of salted water to a boil; drop in dumpling batter 1 tablespoon at a time. Reduce heat to medium-low and simmer, without lifting the lid, until done (about 10 minutes). Remove with a slotted spoon.

Makes about 10 dumplings.

Menu

NEW YEAR'S OPEN HOUSE

Black Bean Soup

Elizabeth's Turkey Soup

Greek Avgolemono Soup

Ham and Gruyère on Croissants

Bacon, Tomato, and Cheese Toasts

Waldorf Salad

Greek Salad

Pound Cake With Lemon Sauce

Chocolate Mousse Pie

Crêpes With Three Jams

For this casual kitchen buffet supper for 16 to 20 people, make the turkey and black bean soups ahead and freeze them; prepare the broth for the Greek soup and the desserts ahead; and assemble the cheese toasts and stack them, covered, until ready to cook.

BLACK BEAN SOUP

2 cups black beans
1 turkey carcass
1 medium onion, finely chopped
4 stalks celery, finely chopped
2 medium carrots, finely chopped
3 tablespoons butter
3 tablespoons flour
Salt
Freshly ground black pepper

1. *A day in advance:* Wash beans and soak overnight in water to cover. The following day, drain beans, reserving liquid as well.

2. In an 8-quart stockpot or Dutch oven, add enough water to reserved bean liquid to make a total of 10 cups. Add beans and turkey carcass.

3. Bring to a boil, then simmer, partially covered, over medium-low heat for 2½ hours. During the last 30 minutes, add onion, celery, and carrots.

4. Remove turkey carcass and discard. Let soup cool.

5. Purée in a food mill, a blender, or food processor. Pour soup back into pot.

6. In a small, heavy-bottomed saucepan over medium heat, melt butter. Whisk in flour, cooking until just golden. Pour 2 cups soup into flour-butter mixture. Whisk until blended. Pour this mixture back into pot; stir to blend well. Season with salt and pepper to taste. Heat through and serve.

Makes 10 cups.

Menu for a relaxed party: The soups sit over low heat on the stove, and the rest of the meal is arranged on counters for guests to help themselves.

ELIZABETH'S TURKEY SOUP

16 cups Turkey Stock (see page 91)
 6 large onions, finely chopped
 1 bunch celery, finely chopped
 1 cup barley
 ¾ cup butter
 ¾ cup flour
 6 cups whipping cream
   Salt and freshly ground black pepper

1. In an 8-quart stockpot or Dutch oven over medium-high heat, bring stock to a boil. Add onions, celery, and barley. Reduce heat to medium-low and simmer until vegetables and barley are tender (about 25 minutes).

2. In a medium, heavy-bottomed saucepan over medium-high heat, melt butter. Add flour, whisking and cooking until golden. Pour in whipping cream, whisking continuously until sauce is smooth and velvety.

3. Slowly pour cream sauce into soup, whisking to blend. Season with salt and pepper.

Makes 16 cups.

GREEK AVGOLEMONO SOUP

 1 whole chicken (about 4 lbs), washed and cleaned
   Salt and freshly ground black pepper
 3 eggs, separated
   Juice of 4 lemons
 3 to 4 cups cooked white rice

1. Put chicken in an 8-quart stockpot or Dutch oven. Cover with cold water; add salt and pepper to taste.

2. Bring to a boil, reduce heat to medium-low, and simmer about 1 hour. Remove chicken and reserve for another use. Ladle out 1½ cups broth and set aside to cool.

3. With an electric mixer beat egg whites in a medium bowl until soft peaks form. Slowly pour in cooled broth, beating continuously. Add lemon juice slowly, then egg yolks, beating continuously.

4. Pour mixture back into pot, whisking to blend. Add rice and gently heat through.

Makes 16 cups.

HAM AND GRUYÈRE ON CROISSANTS

16 croissants
 2 cups chutney
 4 pounds Black Forest ham, thinly sliced
 2 pounds Gruyère cheese, thinly sliced
 2 heads red leaf lettuce, separated, washed, and dried

1. Slice croissants in half horizontally. Spread chutney on inside top and bottom of each croissant.

2. Layer bottom half of each croissant with ham, cheese, and lettuce. Cover with croissant top. Slice sandwiches in half, and arrange on a serving platter.

Makes 16 sandwiches.

BACON, TOMATO, AND CHEESE TOASTS

 1 loaf (1 lb) sweet French bread, cut in ¾-inch-thick slices (about 16 slices)
 1 cup Mayonnaise (see page 107)
 8 slices bacon, cooked and cut in half
 4 tomatoes, thinly sliced
32 thin slices sharp Cheddar cheese (½ to ¾ lb)

1. Preheat broiler. Place bread slices on broiler rack; toast 5 inches from heat on one side only until golden brown (about 2 minutes). Remove from broiler.

2. On untoasted side of each slice, spread a thin layer of mayonnaise. Cover with a half-slice of bacon, 2 to 3 tomato slices, and 2 slices of cheese.

3. Place sandwiches on broiler rack; broil 5 inches from heat until cheese is melted and bubbling (about 4 minutes).

Makes about 16 open-face sandwiches.

WALDORF SALAD

 3 pounds ripe, firm, red eating apples, cored and diced
 ⅓ cup lemon juice
 3 cups sliced celery
 1½ cups coarsely chopped walnuts
 1½ cups Mayonnaise (see page 107)
 3 heads Bibb lettuce, washed and shredded

1. In a medium bowl combine apples and lemon juice; toss to coat.

2. Add celery, walnuts, and mayonnaise. Toss until well blended. Serve on a bed of shredded lettuce.

Serves 16.

GREEK SALAD

 2 small heads romaine lettuce, washed and torn into 2-inch pieces
 8 small tomatoes, sliced in ½-inch wedges
 1 red onion, sliced into rings
 1 pound feta cheese, crumbled
 1 pound green Kalamata olives

Vinaigrette Dressing

 1 cup extra-virgin olive oil
 ⅓ cup red wine vinegar
 2 teaspoons dried thyme
 ½ teaspoon salt
 ½ teaspoon freshly ground black pepper

1. In a large bowl combine lettuce, tomatoes, onion, cheese, and olives. Toss to mix.

2. Prepare Vinaigrette Dressing. Pour over salad and toss to coat.

Serves 16.

Vinaigrette Dressing In a small bowl whisk together oil, vinegar, thyme, salt, and pepper until well blended.

Makes about 1⅓ cups.

POUND CAKE WITH LEMON SAUCE

- ½ pound unsalted butter
- 2 cups sugar
- 6 eggs
- 1 cup sifted all-purpose flour
- 1 cup cake flour
- 1 tablespoon lemon extract

Lemon Sauce

- 2 cups water
- ½ cup sugar
- 2 tablespoons cornstarch
- 6 tablespoons butter
- 4 to 6 tablespoons fresh lemon juice
- 1 teaspoon grated lemon rind

1. Preheat oven to 325° F. Grease and flour a bundt pan.

2. In large bowl of electric mixer, cream butter and sugar together. Blend in eggs. Add flours and extract. Beat on medium speed 10 minutes.

3. Pour batter into prepared pan and bake in center of middle rack of oven until knife inserted in center of cake comes out clean (about 1 to 1½ hours). Cool in pan 10 minutes, invert onto a wire rack, and cool completely.

4. Prepare Lemon Sauce. Pour sauce over slices of pound cake.

Serves 10.

Lemon Sauce In a small saucepan combine water, sugar, and cornstarch. Cook over medium-high heat until thickened. Remove from heat and stir in butter, lemon juice, and lemon rind.

Makes about 3 cups.

CHOCOLATE MOUSSE PIE

- 1 package (8 oz) chocolate wafers, finely crushed
- ½ cup unsalted butter, melted
- 8 ounces bittersweet baking chocolate
- 4 eggs, separated
- 1½ cups whipping cream
- ¼ cup orange-flavored liqueur
  Chocolate shavings
  Sweetened whipped cream flavored with orange-flavored liqueur

1. *At least 9 hours in advance:* In a medium bowl combine crumbs with melted butter. Stir and toss until crumbs are well coated. Press crumb mixture into bottom of a 10-inch springform pan. Chill for at least 20 minutes.

2. Melt chocolate in a double boiler over hot (not boiling) water; set aside to cool to lukewarm.

3. In a small bowl beat egg yolks until pale yellow. In a medium bowl beat egg whites until stiff. In another medium bowl beat the 1½ cups whipping cream until soft peaks form.

4. When chocolate is lukewarm, stir in liqueur, whisking vigorously to blend. Add egg yolks, whisking slowly to blend. Add egg whites, folding gently to blend.

5. Fold in one fourth of the unsweetened whipped cream. Add remaining unsweetened whipped cream and continue folding until completely blended.

6. Pour chocolate mousse mixture over chilled crust. Refrigerate until firm (about 8 hours). Serve in thin slices with chocolate shavings and sweetened whipped cream.

Serves 12 to 16.

CRÊPES WITH THREE JAMS

- 2 cups cake or all-purpose flour
- ⅛ teaspoon salt
- 6 eggs, lightly beaten
- 2 to 3 cups milk
- ½ cup butter, melted

Fillings

- 1 jar (12 oz) lingonberry jam
- 1 jar (12 oz) apricot jam
- 1 jar (12 oz) damson plum preserves
- 1 cup confectioners' sugar

1. Sift flour and salt together into a large bowl. Make a well in the center of the flour and pour eggs into well. Pour in half the milk, and blend flour and milk with a wooden spoon. When these ingredients are combined, add ¼ cup of the melted butter, and beat batter vigorously until smooth and without lumps. Let stand at room temperature for 30 minutes.

2. Add enough more milk to bring batter to consistency of light cream.

3. Preheat a 6-inch skillet or crêpe pan over medium-high heat. Brush with some of the remaining melted butter. When butter is hot, spoon in about 1½ tablespoons batter (enough to lightly cover bottom of skillet). Cook until brown on one side, then turn and brown second side (about 1 minute per side).

4. Remove to platter to cool. Continue until all batter is used, adding butter for each crêpe.

5. *To assemble:* Put crêpes on a platter. Have jams and confectioners' sugar available in separate bowls, with spoons for serving. Have guests assemble their own crêpes, spreading jam on crêpe, rolling it, and sprinkling it with confectioners' sugar.

Makes 30 crêpes.

Based on a vegetable purée, Watercress Sauce (see page 105) is thickened by a cream-stock reduction. The result is a light, fresh, nouvelle-style sauce that seems to be the essence of watercress. It's good with poached poultry.

SAUCES: PERFECT FOR POULTRY

Perhaps no two foods complement one another better than properly prepared, juicy poultry and a velvety-smooth sauce. Sauces for poultry range from simple turkey gravy made from flour-thickened pan drippings to elegant cream-based sauces that are the glory of Western cooking. Sauces are the backbone of classic French cuisine. From five basic "mother" sauces are derived hundreds of variations—an additional ingredient, another garnish, creates a new sauce with a new name. In recent years chefs have added to these classics lighter, more intensely flavored sauces thickened with vegetable reductions.

Just as a soup is a liquid food, a sauce can be considered a liquid seasoning that adds zest and a finishing touch to the food it accompanies. Most often, sauces have a stock or a cream base. However, more broadly defined, a sauce is any fluid dressing, including relishes and condiments.

WHY SAUCE?

An exquisite sauce has always been the hallmark of fine cuisine and the test of a cook's expertise. A well-made sauce is frankly impressive although it may actually be easily and quickly prepared. It implies luxury and competence and mastery of a revered culinary art. Most of all, however, sauces are a treat to the palate, in both flavor and texture. So even though cooking may be evolving to a lighter style, sauces will remain— although today they are more likely to be the flavored butters and fresh vegetable sauces appropriate to simple grilled, broiled, or sautéed poultry rather than the more complex white and brown sauces.

Sauce-making is extremely creative and satisfying. Familiarity with a few basic sauces and how they can be varied will provide a world of choices to the cook and many excellent meals to dinner guests.

Which Sauce to Prepare?

With so many possibilities, the choice of which sauce to use depends on the cook's taste, the occasion, or the character of the meal. Simple pan sauces, concentrates of poultry drippings mixed with other liquids and seasonings, are less formal than cream sauces. A thickened white sauce such as the classic béchamel, on the other hand, doesn't carry the meat's flavor, but serves as a compatible companion to the cooked poultry. A stock-based sauce, such as velouté, will have some meat flavor but not as much as one made with pan drippings.

Other sauces that work well with most poultry preparations include the familiar tomato sauce, fragrant pesto, crème fraîche, compound butters, mayonnaise, and vegetable reductions.

Sauce Ingredients and Thickening Agents

A sauce is a blend of a liquid and flavoring, plus an ingredient that adds body and texture—a thickening agent. Although a sauce intended for use with poultry can be the bird's own juices, a slightly thickened sauce that has enough body to coat the poultry is usually more appealing. You will want to choose a thickener appropriate to the sauce (see page 104). If translucency is essential, as in Oriental sauces, use cornstarch or arrowroot; flour will produce an opaque sauce. For richness use a *roux*, a cooked mixture of flour and butter, or *beurre manié*, equal amounts of flour and butter kneaded together.

Sometimes an enrichment, such as butter and cream, is blended in with the thickening agent. Enrichments do not add texture, but impart a luxurious finish, both visually and to the taste. Egg yolks function as both a thickener and an enrichment.

TIPS FOR SUCCESSFUL SAUCES

A superb sauce—flavorful, luxuriantly textured, perfectly seasoned—is the hallmark of fine cuisine. For many cooks, sauce-making is thus the supreme challenge. Because of this apprehension, the process is surrounded by a mystique that suggests that what happens in the saucepan is often beyond the cook's control. In fact, the process is understandable. These tips will help keep it under control.

☐ Use a heavy-bottomed saucepan, essential for heat conduction. Avoid aluminum or cast iron, as these materials will discolor your sauce.

☐ Use a wooden spoon or whisk for stirring. A whisk will help to prevent lumps.

☐ Give the sauce your constant attention. In particular, watch out for overheating, which will cause it to break down. Stir constantly to prevent the sauce from burning, browning, and sticking to the pan.

☐ Use neutral fats—not olive oil or strong animal fats—especially with delicate sauces. Butter or clarified butter (see page 59) works best; you may substitute margarine, but it will not produce a truly rich-flavored sauce. For gravy, use the fat that has collected in the roasting pan for better flavor.

☐ *To prevent lumping:* When adding liquid to a flour thickener, including roux, have the liquid hot, or whisk vigorously. Always add flour or cornstarch in paste form (mixed with liquid). To fix a sauce that has become lumpy, whisk vigorously, blend it in a blender or food processor, or strain it through a sieve.

☐ If you need to thin an overly thick sauce, use a liquid appropriate to the sauce. Wine, stock, and milk are all commonly used. Gently stir into sauce.

☐ If you need to thicken a too-thin sauce, use beads of beurre manié (see "Thickeners for Sauces and Soups," page 104) or add a paste of flour and water whisked in at the last minute.

☐ If you prefer a smooth sauce without any browned bits or specks of herbs, strain the sauce through a fine sieve before serving.

☐ *To hold a sauce:* A sauce held for hours will develop a crust on the surface. A layer of melted butter or cover of plastic wrap laid directly on the surface of the resting sauce will prevent this undesirable skin. To hold a sauce for two or three days, cover the sauce and refrigerate. Sauces can be frozen in a plastic container for up to three months. Reheat all sauces gently over low heat.

THICKENERS FOR SAUCES AND SOUPS

The same thickeners are employed for both sauces and soups. Listed below are the most commonly used thickening agents and enrichments. Where appropriate, guidelines are offered for both sauces and soups.

Cornstarch produces a translucent sauce with a glossy finish and is a familiar ingredient in Oriental cuisine. To avoid lumping, always add cornstarch in paste form—mixed with liquid. To thicken 1 cup of liquid, mix 1 tablespoon cornstarch with 2 tablespoons water.

Flour is one of the most familiar thickeners. Although cornstarch is close to a pure starch, flour contains insoluble proteins that make the sauce opaque. Flour should also be added as a paste, and then the sauce should be allowed to simmer a few minutes; uncooked flour imparts a strong, undesirable cereal taste. To thicken 1 cup of liquid, mix 2 tablespoons flour with 2 tablespoons water.

Roux, the most common thickener, is equal parts of flour and butter cooked over medium heat to form a paste. One of the secrets of successful sauce-making is a properly cooked roux. The combination of butter and flour adds body and flavor to sauces and soups. The paste can be used immediately, or stored in the refrigerator up to 2 weeks. There are three kinds of roux: white, blond, and brown. White roux is barely cooked,

just enough to remove the taste of the flour. It is used in cream sauces. Blond roux is cooked to a pale golden color and is used in sauces where a white color is not as essential. Brown roux is cooked to a nutty color and used for brown and flavorful sauces. In making roux, heat the butter carefully, or use clarified butter (see page 59). Do not let it brown or burn. When adding the flour, whisk vigorously to blend. It will take about 2 to 3 minutes over medium heat to cook out the flour taste. For a soup, use 1 tablespoon butter and 1 tablespoon flour to thicken 1 cup of liquid. For a sauce, use 2 tablespoons butter and 2 tablespoons flour to thicken 1 cup of liquid.

Beurre manié is an uncooked paste of equal amounts of butter and flour used to build up sauces that are too thin. To make the beurre manié, knead the flour and butter together with fingers, or mash with a fork or spoon. For a soup, use 1 tablespoon flour and 1 tablespoon butter to thicken 1 cup of liquid. For a sauce, use 2 tablespoons flour and 2 tablespoons butter to thicken 1 cup of liquid. Extra beurre manié can be stored, wrapped in waxed paper, in the refrigerator about 10 days.

Whipping cream by itself is considered to be a thickener and an enrichment. A cream reduction is one of the preferred thickening agents for sauces in what is called *nouvelle cuisine*. For soups, add cream at the end of cooking, in whatever amount produces the desired flavor and consistency.

Egg yolks and cream in combination act as both thickener and enrichment. For sauces, mix 1 egg yolk with 2 to 3 tablespoons whipping cream for 1 cup prepared sauce that is already somewhat thick. If the sauce is quite thin, 2 to 3 yolks may be needed to thicken sufficiently.

Pour a little of the hot sauce into the combined yolk and cream and whisk to blend. Pour this mixture back into the sauce and gently heat. Do not allow it to boil or it will curdle. To thicken 6 cups of soup, use 2 egg yolks and ¼ cup of whipping cream. Proceed as for a sauce.

Vegetable purées are used with soups in place of roux to provide a unique taste. These purées add bulk so that another thickener is usually not required. However, cream is often added to a vegetable-purée-based soup for richness. Examples of purées include: bean (such as lentil, black bean, and split pea), tomato, carrot, cucumber, zucchini, potato, and leek. The quantity of purée needed to thicken a soup varies with the vegetable; add it in small amounts until the desired consistency is achieved.

Reduction is a process, not an ingredient, whereby a sauce is slowly simmered over low heat until its volume decreases and its flavor is greatly concentrated. Cooks in a hurry should avoid reduced sauces, although the patient sauce-maker will be rewarded with a bonus of extra flavor. Straining is necessary at times to produce a smooth sauce. Seasoning should be added after reducing as flavor also will intensify as the sauce cooks down. The reduction process is also used to produce a sauce from a vegetable purée; the purée alone is cooked down to produce an intense yet light flavor.

Butter swirls are used mostly as a finish although they will thicken the sauce or soup slightly. Add bits of butter to the sauce at the end of cooking and swirl in the pan to create a spiral. Do not stir. One or two tablespoons will be enough to finish most sauces.

PAN GRAVY FOR POULTRY

To make this elementary and very useful sauce, the pan drippings are first degreased and then thickened with a roux. For a translucent gravy, dissolve a tablespoon of cornstarch into ½ cup of poultry stock or wine. Add this mixture to 1½ cups pan juices instead of the roux.

> 2 cups Poultry Stock (see
> page 91) or a combination of
> Poultry Stock and wine
> Pan drippings from poultry
> ¼ cup butter
> ¼ cup flour
> Salt and freshly ground
> black pepper

1. After bird is removed from roasting pan, skim fat with a spoon. Pour stock into the pan and blend with pan drippings, stirring and scraping with a wooden spoon to loosen any browned bits that may have stuck to the pan.

2. In a heavy-bottomed skillet over medium heat, melt butter. Reduce heat and quickly whisk in flour. Return heat to medium and cook butter and flour until golden (about 2 minutes).

3. Add stock and pan drippings, whisking rapidly until gravy is thoroughly blended and smooth. Season with salt and pepper.

Makes 2 cups.

WATERCRESS SAUCE

To wash the watercress easily, place it in a sink filled with cold water. Move the greens around in the water with your hand. Any dirt will fall to the bottom of the sink, and the watercress will float on the water's surface. To stem, hold the base of the watercress in one hand. With the other hand, pull along the stem. All the leaves on one stem will come off with this one movement.

> 8 cups water with 2 tablespoons
> salt
> 1 bunch watercress, washed and
> stemmed (stems discarded)
> 1 shallot, minced
> ¼ cup dry vermouth
> ½ cup Chicken Stock (see
> page 91)
> 1 cup whipping cream
> 1 tablespoon minced green
> onion
> ½ cup butter, softened
> Salt and white pepper

1. In a medium saucepan bring salted water to a boil. Blanch watercress leaves in boiling water for 10 seconds; remove with a slotted spoon into a bowl of ice water. After 10 seconds, remove leaves from ice water and squeeze out all moisture. Put watercress in a blender and purée.

2. In a small saucepan combine shallot and vermouth. Bring to a boil and simmer until vermouth has evaporated. Remove from heat.

3. In another small saucepan combine Chicken Stock and cream. Bring to a boil over medium-high heat; reduce heat to medium-low and simmer until cream is reduced by one third (about 7 minutes). Remove from heat.

4. In a blender combine watercress, shallot, green onion, and butter; purée. Pour in cream and purée until smooth and velvety (about 30 to 60 seconds). Season to taste.

5. Pour sauce into a small saucepan, heat through, and serve.

Makes 1 cup.

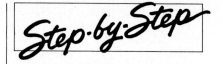

HOW TO MAKE PAN GRAVY

Pan gravy is one of the basic sauces. Made with the drippings from the cooked bird, it is rich with the flavor of the poultry.

1. *Skim fat from drippings, then blend stock into drippings, stirring and scraping with wooden spoon to loosen any browned bits that have stuck to the pan.*

2. *To prepare roux, melt butter, whisk in flour, and cook until golden. Add stock and pan drippings to roux and cook, whisking rapidly, until gravy is thoroughly blended and smooth.*

One of the classics of French cuisine, béchamel is the base of many sauces. Made with milk or cream, it is white, smooth, and rich enough to be pleasurable in itself—over fish, poultry, or vegetables—yet adaptable enough to accept many other flavorings; see the variations listed at right.

BÉCHAMEL SAUCE

A *béchamel* is a classic French white or cream sauce usually made with milk and a white roux. It is used either by itself or as a base for many other sauces. For example, a Mornay sauce blends béchamel with grated cheese. A curry sauce is curry mixed with béchamel. This recipe uses half-and-half instead of milk for a richer flavor.

> 2 tablespoons butter
> 2 tablespoons flour
> 1 cup half-and-half (or milk)
>   Salt and white pepper

1. In a 1-quart saucepan over medium heat, melt butter. Quickly whisk in flour and cook mixture briefly (about 1 minute).

2. Reduce heat and add half-and-half, whisking rapidly until sauce is thoroughly blended and smooth. Season with salt and pepper.

Makes 1 cup.

VELOUTÉ SAUCE

Velouté is a white sauce made with stock. A tasty, well-flavored poultry stock produces a quality sauce. Like béchamel, velouté is a basic preparation and has many variations. Sauce Bercy, for example, is a shallot-flavored velouté.

> 2 tablespoons butter
> 2 tablespoons flour
> 1 cup Poultry Stock (see page 91)
>   Salt and white pepper

1. In a 1-quart saucepan over medium heat, melt butter. Quickly whisk in flour and cook until mixture becomes golden (about 2 minutes).

2. Reduce heat and add stock, whisking rapidly until sauce is thoroughly blended and smooth. Season with salt and pepper.

Makes 1 cup.

VARIATIONS ON BÉCHAMEL SAUCE AND VELOUTÉ SAUCE

Practical experience is the best cooking teacher. Starting with these two basic sauces, try any of the following variations, or experiment to create your own. Each is based on 1 cup of prepared sauce.

To 1 cup of either sauce, add:

☐ 3 tablespoons whipping cream combined with 1 egg yolk

☐ 1 tablespoon curry powder

☐ 3 tablespoons minced fresh herbs (tarragon, chervil, parsley, basil)

☐ 1 to 2 tablespoons Dijon mustard

To 1 cup of Béchamel Sauce, add:

☐ ⅓ cup grated Swiss cheese; stir over low heat to melt and blend

☐ ¼ cup freshly grated Parmesan cheese; stir over low heat to melt and blend

To 1 cup of Velouté Sauce, add:

- ¼ cup white wine or dry vermouth combined with the poultry stock
- 1 tablespoon Cognac or brandy (or to taste)
- 2 tablespoons shallots as the butter is melting, before adding flour to make the roux
- ¼ cup thinly sliced mushrooms. For additional flavor, add 1 teaspoon minced chanterelles or cèpes
- 1 to 2 tablespoons capers

HOLLANDAISE

Not a stock- or cream-based sauce, hollandaise is an emulsion of egg yolks, melted butter, and lemon juice. Hollandaise can be tricky, breaking easily. Some hints: Remove the sauce from the heat before adding the butter; too much heat will break the sauce. Pour the butter in slowly. If it is added too fast, the egg yolks will not be able to absorb the fat quickly enough and the sauce will be runny. If your sauce breaks, try one of these remedies:

- Beat in cold whipping cream, a tablespoon at a time, until the sauce is reconstituted.
- Beat together 1 teaspoon lemon juice with a tablespoon of sauce in a warm bowl until thickened. Add the broken sauce, a tablespoon at a time, whisking constantly until the sauce is reconstituted.

Hollandaise can be held up to 45 minutes in a double boiler set on a warming tray. To use hollandaise with poultry, try a Sauce Mousseline, which is a hollandaise enriched with whipping cream, or mix chopped fresh tomatoes into room-temperature hollandaise and serve over cold poached chicken breasts.

3 egg yolks
4 tablespoons boiling water
1½ tablespoons lemon juice, warmed
½ cup butter, melted and kept warm
Salt
Cayenne pepper

1. In a double boiler over simmering water, beat egg yolks with a whisk until they begin to thicken.

2. Add 1 tablespoon of the boiling water to egg yolks and beat again to thicken. Repeat with remaining 3 tablespoons of boiling water.

3. Beat in lemon juice. Remove double boiler from heat.

4. Slowly pour in melted butter, about a tablespoon at a time, whisking continuously until sauce is thick and fluffy. Season with salt and cayenne pepper. Serve at once, or hold as directed above.

Makes 1 cup.

BLENDER HOLLANDAISE

Using a blender to prepare hollandaise sauce makes a more stable emulsion, but the sauce will lack some of the body and flavor of the traditional preparation. To improve the texture, reheat over low heat until thickened slightly.

3 egg yolks
2 tablespoons boiling water
½ cup butter, melted and kept warm
1 tablespoon lemon juice, warmed
½ teaspoon salt
Dash cayenne pepper

1. Put egg yolks in a blender or food processor. Turn blender on medium-high speed, wait a few seconds, and add boiling water, blending a few seconds more.

2. Pour butter into eggs in a slow, steady stream. Add lemon juice, salt, and cayenne pepper. Whirl for a few seconds to blend.

Makes about ¾ cup.

MAYONNAISE

Similar to hollandaise in its use and preparation, mayonnaise is always served cold. It is a wonderful dressing for poultry salads, and when fortified with additional mustard, is the perfect accompaniment to hot or cold fried chicken. To avoid a soupy mayonnaise, pour the oil into the eggs very slowly. Beat with a hand-held electric beater or a balloon whisk.

1 egg
1 egg yolk
2 tablespoons tarragon vinegar
½ teaspoon salt
¼ teaspoon Dijon mustard
⅛ teaspoon white pepper
Pinch sugar
2 cups extra-virgin olive oil

1. In a large bowl mix together egg, egg yolk, vinegar, salt, mustard, pepper, and sugar.

2. Slowly pour in oil, about ½ teaspoon at a time, beating continuously. Continue until ¼ cup of oil is used.

3. Slowly beat in remaining oil, approximately a tablespoon at a time. Correct seasonings. Refrigerate until ready to use.

Makes 2 cups.

Aïoli Add 4 to 8 cloves crushed garlic to egg mixture before adding the oil.

Green Mayonnaise To finished sauce add ¼ cup fresh minced herbs, such as tarragon, chives, dill, basil, or chervil, or a mixture of these.

Pimiento For color add 1 small jar drained chopped pimiento to finished sauce.

Mustard To finished sauce add ½ cup Dijon mustard, 4 cloves crushed garlic, and ¼ cup white wine vinegar. Blend.

CRÈME FRAÎCHE

Crème fraîche is a cultured cream that the French often use in sauces. It can be substituted, one for one, for whipping cream or sour cream in any recipe. It has a light taste and does not curdle when cooked over high heat. It can be stored in the refrigerator for up to two weeks.

> 1 cup whipping cream
> 2 tablespoons buttermilk, sour cream, or leftover Crème Fraîche

1. In a small bowl combine whipping cream with buttermilk.

2. Cover and set in a warm spot until thick, anywhere from 8 hours to 2 days. When it is thickened, refrigerate until ready to use.

Makes 1 cup.

Tomato Sauce Combine 1 cup Fresh Tomato Sauce (at right) and ½ cup Crème Fraîche.

Mustard Sauce Combine 1 cup Crème Fraîche with ½ cup Dijon mustard and ½ cup chopped chives.

PESTO

Fragrant with sweet basil and pungent garlic, pesto is a versatile Italian sauce with a concentrated, full flavor. A little goes a long way: 2 to 4 tablespoons of pesto will sauce one portion of poultry. Pesto can be refrigerated up to a month, or frozen for several months.

> 2 bunches fresh basil
> 3 cloves garlic, crushed
> ¾ cup pine nuts
> 2 cups freshly grated Parmesan cheese
> 1¼ cups extra-virgin olive oil

1. Wash and dry basil carefully, separating leaves from stems. Discard stems. Put leaves in a mortar and pound until finely ground. Add garlic and pine nuts, and continue to pound until well mixed.

2. In a medium bowl combine grated Parmesan and basil mixture; stir until a thick mixture results.

3. Slowly pour in olive oil, stirring constantly. When pesto is thoroughly mixed, pour it into a container. Use immediately or store in refrigerator or freezer. For refrigerator storage, pour a layer of oil over top of pesto to prevent its discoloring.

Makes about 3½ cups.

BLENDER PESTO

> 2 bunches fresh basil
> 3 cloves garlic, crushed
> ¾ cup pine nuts
> 2 cups freshly grated Parmesan cheese
> 1¼ cups extra-virgin olive oil

1. Wash and dry basil carefully, separating leaves from stems. Discard stems. Put leaves into a blender or bowl of food processor fitted with a metal blade. Add garlic, pine nuts, and grated Parmesan. Process until mixture is well blended.

2. With machine on, slowly pour in olive oil in a steady stream. When pesto is thoroughly mixed, pour it into a container. Use immediately or store in refrigerator or freezer. For refrigerator storage, pour a layer of oil over top of pesto to prevent its discoloring.

Makes 3½ cups.

FRESH TOMATO SAUCE

Everyone loves a good tomato sauce. Use this one hot or cold over poultry.

> 6 large ripe tomatoes, peeled and seeded (see Note)
> ½ cup extra-virgin olive oil
> 3 shallots, minced
> 1 teaspoon dried thyme
> 1 teaspoon dried oregano
> 1 teaspoon dried tarragon
> 1 teaspoon ground cinnamon
> 1 teaspoon salt
> ⅛ teaspoon freshly ground black pepper

1. By hand or in a food processor, chop tomatoes finely.

2. In a 2-quart, heavy-bottomed saucepan, combine olive oil, shallot, thyme, oregano, tarragon, cinnamon, salt, and pepper. Cook over medium heat until warmed through (about 2 minutes).

3. Add tomatoes, stirring to combine. Cover and cook over low heat 15 to 20 minutes; taste and correct seasonings, if necessary. Serve hot or cold over poultry.

Makes 4 cups.

Note If ripe fresh tomatoes are not available, substitute 1 can (28 oz) peeled Italian plum tomatoes.

Fresh Tomato Cream Sauce

> 1 cup Fresh Tomato Sauce
> ½ cup whipping cream

In a small saucepan combine tomato sauce and cream. Cook over medium heat until heated through (about 5 minutes).

Makes 1½ cups.

COMPOUND BUTTERS

Compound butters are a simple mix of butter and flavoring used to sauce grilled and broiled poultry, and wonderful for basting as well. Compound butters should be made in quantity. They freeze well, up to two months wrapped in waxed paper, and will always be on hand for a special finish. Shape the butter into a block before freezing. To use, cut the desired amount off the block and store the remainder. Prepare the butters as follows: In a medium bowl combine the ingredients either by hand or with an electric mixer until well blended. Use immediately, or wrap in waxed paper and refrigerate or freeze.

Orange Butter

½ cup butter, softened
2 teaspoons freshly squeezed
   orange juice
   Grated rind of 1 orange

Makes ½ cup.

Watercress Butter

½ cup butter, softened
½ cup watercress leaves, minced

Makes ½ cup.

Blue Cheese Butter

2 tablespoons butter, softened
2 tablespoons cream cheese,
   softened
2 tablespoons blue cheese,
   softened

Makes ⅓ cup.

Lemon Butter

½ cup butter, softened
2 tablespoons freshly squeezed
   lemon juice
   Grated rind of 1 lemon

Makes ½ cup.

Shallot Butter

½ cup butter, softened
½ cup minced shallots

Makes ½ cup.

Cilantro Butter

¼ cup butter, softened
½ cup chopped cilantro

Makes ⅓ cup.

Herbed Butter

½ cup butter, softened
2 tablespoons minced parsley
1 tablespoon snipped fresh
   chives
1 clove garlic, crushed

Makes ½ cup.

Hot Chile Butter

½ cup butter, softened
1 teaspoon minced fresh green
   chile
   Few drops hot-pepper sauce

Makes ½ cup.

There is no comparison between homemade Fresh Tomato Sauce and its commercial counterpart. Prepare it in quantity, some to use now and the rest to freeze.

Special-occasion dishes, pâtés are wonderfully rich "meat loaves" with luxurious flavor and texture. Pictured here is Pâté Maison, page 124.

Celebrating the Cooked Bird

Three cheers for the pleasures of the cooked bird! This chapter celebrates it from beginning—three menus for entertaining (see pages 114-121)— to end: recipes for leftovers, both tidbits of cooked poultry (see pages 122-124) and those sometimes forgotten little nuggets of velvety flavor, chicken livers (see "Pâtés and Terrines," pages 124-125). There are also tips on entertaining (see page 112) and step-by-step instructions for carving a turkey (see page 113).

SPECIAL CELEBRATIONS

We eat to stay alive. When we dine, however, enjoying what Brillat-Savarin described as "the pleasures of the table"—carefully prepared food, in a convivial atmosphere, with congenial companions—we experience one of life's great satisfactions.

Dining needn't be a complicated orchestration of white linen, fine china, massive floral arrangements, and a soup-to-nuts menu, although on occasion such formal elegance is appropriate and appreciated. Success at the table is more often the result of the cook's desire to please the guests, to make them feel comfortable and welcome, independent of the simplicity or elaborateness of the preparations. Good food, whether a plate of easily assembled sandwiches of leftover turkey on homemade biscuits or the more sophisticated sautéed quail in a ruby-colored currant sauce, is the foundation of a memorable event. But planning is essential. With every task considered, every preparation technique understood, and all tasks broken down to manageable steps, the cook will be serenely in control. The result will be more time spent with guests, which is, after all, what entertaining is all about.

HOLIDAYS AND PARTIES: PLANNING IS THE KEY

Entertaining should appear as effortless as possible. The ideal is a festive, yet relaxed, ambience in which guest and host spend as much time together as possible. Whether the occasion is a simple and casual supper with a few friends, or a formal Christmas dinner for 20, success will be in direct proportion to the cook's attention to detail. To simplify organizing and make the job appear less formidable, think through the preparation needed for your celebration, compile a list, and follow it step by step.

Consider the following when planning your next celebration:

☐ Plan a menu with as many make-ahead dishes as possible. Even if the actual cooking cannot be done in advance, ingredients can be assembled, measured, and often cut up the night before or early in the day. Don't forget garnishes.

☐ When developing the menu, consider your equipment. Does the kitchen have one or two ovens? Is the refrigerator large or small? How much freezer space is available? If your dessert requires an entire shelf in the refrigerator or freezer, there will be less room to store other dishes or ingredients.

☐ As soon as the menu and guest list are set, start making lists of ingredients to be purchased and tasks to be done.

☐ Your planning should include checking that linens, dishes, flatware, and serving pieces are ready to be used. Give yourself time to polish silver, wash and iron linens, or have dry cleaning done. Consider each course of the menu and be sure that you have the appropriate utensils ready. Set the table the night before the event or that morning, including setting out flowers or other table decorations when possible.

☐ Recognize which tasks can be delegated, and do so when appropriate.

☐ Buffet service cuts down on trips to the kitchen. If you are having a sit-down event, the cook should be seated as close as possible to the serving area to keep an eye on what needs to be refilled or rearranged.

CARVING: AN EASILY MASTERED SKILL

Carving is the process of cutting a whole bird into attractive, serving-sized pieces. Have on hand a carving knife with a long, narrow blade about 8 to 10 inches long and 1 inch wide, made of a material that can be sharpened and that will hold an edge, such as high-carbon stainless steel. Also useful are a two-pronged chef's fork and a carving board with a well.

After removing the bird from the oven, wait to carve it until it has sat for 15 or 20 minutes, depending upon its size. This resting period allows the juices to recirculate and the bird's internal temperature to equalize. As a rule, carve only what is needed. The rest of the meat will stay moist if stored on the frame.

TO CARVE A TURKEY

The ritual of carving the holiday bird need not be an intimidating process. With the proper equipment, even a novice can do a fine job. The procedure shown in the photo sequence on the opposite page is for carving the bird in the kitchen. For carving at the table, remove the legs as shown in step 1, separate the drumstick and the thigh (you may wish to slice the meat off them as well), and slice the breast meat parallel to the backbone in slices about ¼ inch thick. One hint: Have the neck end of the bird facing the carver. When it is positioned this way, the breast meat will be at a better angle for slicing.

TO CARVE A CHICKEN

Differing mainly in size, turkey and chicken are carved almost identically. To carve a chicken, follow the guidelines for turkey (see opposite page), but do not slice the meat on the thigh, drumstick, and breast. Remove the breast meat in one piece by inserting the blade of the knife into the chicken flat along the breastbone.

Follow the contour of the bone with the knife, and the breast half will come away from the frame. After carving you will have two breast halves, two thighs, two drumsticks, and two wings.

TO CARVE A DUCK OR GOOSE

Both ducks and geese have a rectangular, boxy shape, with less breast meat and a higher bone-to-meat ratio than turkey and chicken. Start carving as for the turkey, inserting the point of the knife where the thickest part of the leg meets the breast. Slice down to the joint. Stick the knife directly into the joint and sever the leg from the body. A duck or goose leg joint is tucked under the body and can be hard to locate. If it proves elusive, slit the leg, hold it with one hand and the body with the other hand, and pull them away from each other. The joint will be exposed and the leg will separate from the body. As the leg is less meaty than that of turkey or chicken, do not separate the thigh from the drumstick. Carve the breast as you would a turkey breast. Cut off the wings as for a turkey, but reserve them for stock; they are mostly bone. After carving you will have two legs and the sliced breast meat.

TO CARVE SMALL BIRDS

Rock Cornish game hens and other small birds are served either whole or, if they are large, halved. To halve a game hen, use a sharp knife or poultry shears and make the first cut along the breastbone. Follow this line all the way around the bird.

Eating a whole game hen is a carving operation on a small scale, but one that requires only an ordinary table knife and fork because the bird is so tender. If the hen is stuffed, first remove the stuffing with a spoon, holding the bird in place with a fork. Then, still stabilizing the bird with a fork, slice one leg from the body. Next, cut along the breastbone and pull the breast meat toward you. Turn the bird and repeat with other side.

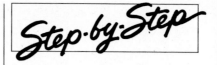

HOW TO CARVE A TURKEY

The technique illustrated here is intended to be done in the kitchen. This method produces sliced meat that can be neatly arranged on a platter, so that guests can help themselves to the portion they prefer. The bones stay in the kitchen, making eating a much neater process. A carving board with a well is the best surface to work on. If yours is made of wood, clean it thoroughly after each use.

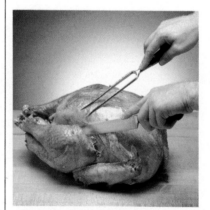

1. *Cut away trussing string and discard it. Insert point of knife into bird where meaty part of leg meets breast, and slice down to the leg joint. Stick knife directly into the joint and sever leg from body. Leg should fall away easily. Repeat on other side.*

2. *Turn leg skin side up. Insert knife through joint and cut to separate drumstick and thigh. Slice meat off drumstick and thigh; arrange meat on serving platter.*

3. *Remove wing by inserting knife at joint where wing joins body. Slice through joint. Transfer to serving platter. Repeat on other side.*

4. *Remove the breast meat in one piece by inserting the blade of the knife into the bird flat along the breastbone. Follow the contour of the bone with the knife, and the breast half will come away from the frame. Repeat with other side. Slice the breast meat and arrange it on serving platter.*

A romantic dinner for two on St. Valentine's Day carries out the holiday motif with toast hearts and red: caviar, apples in the salad, and red currant sauce.

VALENTINE'S DAY DINNER FOR TWO

Red Caviar on Toast Hearts

Sautéed Quail With Red Currant Sauce

Spinach Timbales

Jicama-Apple Salad With Walnut Vinaigrette

Popovers

Biscuit Tortoni

To prepare the meal ahead, bake the timbales in advance and serve them at room temperature, and freeze the biscuit tortoni as much as a week before they are needed. Do not open the oven door to check the popovers while they bake, or they may deflate. Jicama, a crunchy root vegetable used for the salad, is usually available at markets that carry Mexican and South American foods.

RED CAVIAR ON TOAST HEARTS

> 2 slices white bread
> 1 ounce red salmon caviar
> Half a lemon, cut in 2 equal wedges

1. With a 3-inch, heart-shaped cookie cutter, cut out a bread heart from each bread slice. Lightly toast hearts.

2. To serve, spread caviar on toast hearts. Squeeze lemon juice over caviar.

Serves 2.

SAUTÉED QUAIL WITH RED CURRANT SAUCE

> 4 quail
> Salt
> 2 tablespoons butter
> 1 tablespoon oil

Red Currant Sauce

> ¼ cup red currant jelly
> ¼ cup canned gooseberries with juice
> 1 tablespoon red wine vinegar
> ⅛ teaspoon each *ground cinnamon, ground nutmeg, and ground ginger*

1. Wash quail and pat dry; truss. Sprinkle with salt. In a medium, heavy-bottomed sauté pan or skillet over medium-high heat, heat butter and oil.

2. Add quail and sauté until golden brown on all sides (about 4 minutes). Reduce heat to medium-low, cover, and cook until tender (12 to 15 minutes). Remove quail and set aside. Leave drippings in pan for sauce.

3. Prepare Red Currant Sauce. To serve, snip trussing strings on quail and discard. Return quail to sauté pan; pour sauce over quail and warm gently over medium heat for 2 minutes. Arrange birds on serving platter and spoon sauce over.

Serves 2.

Red Currant Sauce In a small bowl combine jelly, gooseberries with juice, vinegar, and spices. Transfer to a small saucepan and cook over medium heat until jelly melts (about 3 minutes). Pour mixture into sauté pan, stirring and scraping with a wooden spoon to loosen any browned bits that may have stuck to the bottom of the pan. Cook over medium heat until heated through.

Makes about ½ cup sauce.

SPINACH TIMBALES

> ½ cup whipping cream, warmed
> 1 egg
> ¼ teaspoon salt
> ⅛ teaspoon mild Hungarian paprika
> Pinch ground nutmeg
> ½ cup cooked, chopped spinach, drained and squeezed dry
> 3 tablespoons freshly grated Parmesan cheese
> 2 tablespoons minced shallot
> 1 tablespoon minced parsley

1. Preheat oven to 325° F. In a medium bowl mix together cream, egg, salt, paprika, and nutmeg. Add spinach, Parmesan cheese, shallots, and parsley. Stir to blend.

2. Generously butter two 1-cup soufflé or timbale molds. Fill molds about two-thirds full with mixture. Place molds in a small glass baking dish. Fill dish with hot water to reach about three fourths of the way up the sides of the molds.

3. Place dish with molds in center of middle rack of oven. Bake until timbales are golden brown and a knife inserted in center comes out clean (20 to 30 minutes).

4. To unmold, run a knife around the inside edge of each mold. Invert molds onto dinner plates, tap sharply with a knife, and lift off. Serve hot or at room temperature.

Makes 2 timbales.

JICAMA-APPLE SALAD WITH WALNUT VINAIGRETTE

⅓ pound jicama, peeled and julienned

Half a Red Delicious apple, cored and julienned

3 tablespoons coarsely chopped walnuts

1 small head Bibb lettuce, washed, dried, and separated into leaves

4 sprigs watercress, washed and dried

Walnut Vinaigrette

¼ cup walnut oil

2 tablespoons sherry vinegar

Pinch sugar

1. Prepare Walnut Vinaigrette. In a medium bowl toss together jicama, apple, and walnuts. Pour Walnut Vinaigrette over mixture and toss to coat.

2. To assemble, arrange lettuce leaves on two salad plates. Mound jicama-apple mixture on lettuce. Garnish with watercress sprigs.

Serves 2.

Walnut Vinaigrette In a small bowl whisk together oil, vinegar, and sugar.

Makes about ⅓ cup.

POPOVERS

½ cup sifted flour

⅛ teaspoon salt

½ cup milk

2 tablespoons butter, melted

1 egg, lightly beaten

1. Preheat oven to 450° F. Butter 2 to 4 of the cups in a muffin tin or popover pan.

2. In a small bowl whisk together flour, salt, milk, and melted butter until smooth. Gently whisk in beaten egg. Fill muffin tins half full with batter.

3. Bake popovers in center of middle rack of oven for 15 minutes. Reduce heat to 350° F; bake another 20 minutes, until puffed and golden brown. Do not open oven door until last 5 minutes of baking time.

Makes 2 to 4 popovers.

BISCUIT TORTONI

½ cup whipping cream

3 tablespoons half-and-half
Pinch salt

3 tablespoons confectioners' sugar

4 coconut macaroons, crushed

2 tablespoons cream sherry

2 long-stemmed strawberries, for garnish

1. About 1 hour before beginning preparations, turn freezer to coldest setting. To prepare tortoni, beat together whipping cream, half-and-half, and salt in a small stainless steel, glass, or ceramic bowl until soft peaks form. Gently fold in sugar with a spatula. Cover bowl with a double layer of aluminum foil and freeze until nearly solid (about 1½ hours).

2. With a fork or wooden spoon, break up frozen mixture. Transfer to a medium bowl. With a wooden spoon gently blend in two thirds of macaroon crumbs and the sherry. Mixture should be of a light consistency.

3. Spoon mixture into two 1-cup soufflé molds. Cover molds with double layer of aluminum foil and return to freezer. Freeze until solid (6 to 8 hours).

4. When tortoni are quite firm, remove from freezer. To unmold, run a knife around inside of mold to loosen tortoni. Invert molds onto a serving platter and wrap with a cloth wrung out in very hot water. Tap each mold and lift off.

5. Press remaining macaroon crumbs lightly onto top and sides of tortoni. Garnish with long-stemmed strawberries. Serve.

Serves 2.

menu

A SUNDAY BRUNCH IN JUNE

Chicken Liver Croustades

Artichoke Frittata With Tomato Coulis

Blueberry Bread With Orange Butter

Mushrooms Stuffed With Herb Cheese

Mixed Fruit With Crème Anglaise

This menu allows the cook to sleep in and still have everything under control. Freeze the bread and orange butter days in advance. The day before, assemble and refrigerate the frittata, the mushrooms, the fruit, and the crème anglaise. Bake the frittata before the guests arrive; broil the mushrooms right from the refrigerator; and bring the fruit and crème anglaise to room temperature before serving.

CHICKEN LIVER CROUSTADES

1⅓ loaves unsliced white
    sandwich bread
⅓ cup butter, melted
1 cup minced shallots
1 pound chicken livers, washed,
    dried, trimmed, and halved
½ pound seedless green
    grapes, washed
⅓ cup pale dry sherry
¼ cup minced parsley

1. Preheat oven to 350° F. Remove crusts from bread. Cut bread crosswise into 8 slices, each 1½ inches thick. Scoop out center of each slice, leaving a ½-inch-thick shell. Press down bottom of shell from inside to create a compact foundation with no holes. Be careful not to tear bread.

2. Place shells on a baking sheet. Brush sides, top, and interior with ¼ cup of the melted butter. Bake in center of middle rack of oven until light golden brown (12 to 15 minutes). Remove and keep warm.

3. *For the filling:* In a large, heavy-bottomed skillet, heat remaining 2 tablespoons butter. Add shallots and sauté over medium-high heat until golden brown (about 5 minutes). Add chicken livers and sauté until livers are golden brown on the outside and pink within (5 to 7 minutes). Add grapes and heat through (about 1 minute). Pour in sherry, stirring to blend.

4. To serve, spoon ⅓ cup chicken livers into each warm croustade. Sprinkle with parsley.

Makes 8 croustades.

Brunch is a relaxing meal that can move outdoors on a warm and sunny June morning. Potted flowers, or whatever is blooming in the garden, can decorate the table.

ARTICHOKE FRITTATA WITH TOMATO COULIS

2 tablespoons butter
1 small clove garlic, minced
1 small onion, sliced
6 eggs
1 can (14 oz) artichoke hearts, drained
  Salt and freshly ground black pepper
  Paprika

Tomato Coulis

¼ cup extra-virgin olive oil
2 shallots, minced
½ teaspoon dried thyme
½ teaspoon dried oregano
½ teaspoon dried tarragon
½ teaspoon ground cinnamon
½ teaspoon salt
3 large ripe tomatoes, peeled, seeded, and finely chopped

1. Preheat oven to 350° F. Butter an 8- by 8-inch baking dish.

2. In a medium, heavy-bottomed skillet over medium heat, melt butter. Add garlic and onion and sauté until soft and translucent.

3. In a medium bowl lightly beat eggs. Stir in artichoke hearts. Add sautéed onion, stirring to mix thoroughly. Season with salt and pepper.

4. Pour egg-artichoke mixture into baking dish. Sprinkle with paprika. Bake, uncovered, until golden brown (about 40 minutes). Serve hot or at room temperature with Tomato Coulis.

Serves 8.

Tomato Coulis In a 2-quart, heavy-bottomed saucepan, combine olive oil, shallots, and seasonings. Cook over medium heat until warmed through (about 2 minutes). Add tomatoes, stirring to blend. Cook, covered, over low heat, 15 to 20 minutes; correct seasonings if necessary. Serve hot or at room temperature with frittata.

Makes 2 cups.

BLUEBERRY BREAD WITH ORANGE BUTTER

2 eggs, lightly beaten
1 cup sugar
¾ cup milk
3 tablespoons butter, melted
3 cups flour
1 tablespoon baking powder
1 teaspoon salt
1 cup fresh or frozen (thawed) blueberries, or 1 can (16½ oz) blueberries, drained
  Orange Butter (see page 109)

1. Preheat oven to 350° F. Grease and flour a 9- by 5-inch loaf pan.

2. In a large bowl blend together eggs, sugar, milk, and butter. Onto a large square of waxed paper, sift together flour, baking powder, and salt. Gradually add sifted dry ingredients to liquid, stirring to blend. Gently fold in blueberries.

3. Pour batter into prepared loaf pan. Bake in center of middle rack of oven until bread is golden brown and a knife inserted in center comes out clean (50 to 60 minutes). Serve with Orange Butter.

Makes 1 loaf.

MUSHROOMS STUFFED WITH HERB CHEESE

1 pound mascarpone cheese
4 small bunches basil, washed and minced to make 2 cups
½ cup pine nuts
16 large mushrooms, stemmed

1. Preheat broiler. In a medium bowl combine cheese and basil. Stir to blend well. Gently fold in pine nuts.

2. Spoon 1 tablespoon cheese mixture into each mushroom cap. Place mushrooms on broiler pan and broil 5 inches from heat until golden brown and heated through (3 to 5 minutes). Serve hot.

Makes 16 stuffed mushrooms.

MIXED FRUIT WITH CRÈME ANGLAISE

3 cups whipping cream
1 cup sugar
8 egg yolks
2 pints strawberries, washed, stemmed, and halved
1 ripe papaya, peeled and sliced into thin wedges
6 kiwi fruits, peeled and sliced

1. *To make crème anglaise:* In a 2-quart, heavy-bottomed saucepan, scald cream over medium heat. Stir in sugar.

2. Place egg yolks in a small bowl. Gradually blend in ½ cup of the hot cream. Pour egg mixture into saucepan with scalded cream. Cook over medium heat, stirring constantly, until cream thickens.

3. In a large bowl combine strawberries, papaya, and kiwi fruit. Toss to blend. To serve, place fruit in serving bowl. Serve crème anglaise in sauce pitcher on the side.

Serves 8.

118

Menu

Christmas in ski country is a charming idea—but cooking an elaborate meal in a tiny vacation-home kitchen could turn the cook into a Scrooge. However, good cheer will abound with this feast, which can be prepared with one oven and a four-burner range.

CREAM OF BROCCOLI SOUP

> 2 heads broccoli, coarsely chopped, about 8 cups
> 4 cups Chicken Stock (see page 91)
> 2 cups whipping cream
> 2 teaspoons salt
> ½ teaspoon freshly ground black pepper
> Croutons, for garnish (see page 97)

1. In a 4-quart saucepan steam broccoli in a steamer over salted water until just tender (about 10 to 12 minutes). Drain.

2. In a blender or food processor, purée broccoli with Chicken Stock in batches. Put purée in saucepan.

3. Bring purée to a boil over medium-high heat. Reduce heat to medium-low. Add cream, whisking to blend, and cook about 2 minutes. Season with salt and pepper. Serve garnished with croutons.

Makes 8 to 10 cups.

BRAISED GOOSE IN HARD CIDER

> 2 stalks celery, coarsely chopped
> 1 carrot, peeled and coarsely chopped
> 1 parsnip, peeled and coarsely chopped
> 1 medium onion, quartered
> 1 goose (about 14 lbs)
> Salt and freshly ground black pepper
> 4 cups hard cider

Pan Gravy

> ¼ cup flour
> 2 cups Goose or Chicken Stock (see page 91)
> Salt and freshly ground black pepper

1. Preheat oven to 450° F. In a large roasting pan place celery, carrot, parsnip, and onion.

2. Remove giblets from goose. Wash goose and pat dry; remove excess fat. Pierce skin of goose several times with the tip of a knife. Sprinkle inside and out with salt and pepper. Tie legs together and set goose on vegetables in roasting pan.

3. Roast in center of middle rack of oven for 30 minutes. Reduce heat to 325° F. After roasting for an additional 1½ hours, pour hard cider into bottom of pan. Roast for 1½ more hours (a total of 3½ hours), or until done to suit. Periodically skim fat from pan with a bulb baster.

4. When goose is done, remove it from oven; allow it to rest 30 minutes before carving. Serve with Pan Gravy.

Serves 12.

Pan Gravy Skim off all but ¼ cup fat from pan juices. Place roasting pan with juices over medium-high heat. Add flour and cook until golden brown, stirring constantly. Add stock, stirring and scraping with a wooden spoon to loosen any browned bits that may have stuck to the bottom of the pan. Cook and stir until texture of gravy is smooth and velvety. Season with salt and pepper.

Makes 3 cups.

LEEK AND CARROT STUFFING

> 6 leeks, white part only, washed and thinly sliced
> 3 cups peeled, trimmed, and halved baby carrots
> 6 cups fresh bread crumbs
> 1½ cups half-and-half
> 1½ cups hard cider
> 2 teaspoons salt, or to taste
> 1 teaspoon freshly ground black pepper, or to taste

1. Preheat oven to 325° F. Butter a 2-quart casserole. In a large bowl combine leeks, carrots, and bread crumbs. Add half-and-half and cider; toss. Season with salt and pepper.

2. Place stuffing in casserole. Bake, covered, in center of middle rack of oven for 1 hour. Remove lid for last 15 minutes to brown top.

Makes 6 cups.

This Christmas feast is designed to be assembled at home, and then transported by cooler in the car. Upon arrival at the cabin in snow country, everything but the goose and the stuffing can be finished on top of the stove. Recipes start on page 119.

MAPLE-PECAN YAMS

> 5 *pounds yams*
> ¼ *teaspoon salt*
> 3 *tablespoons butter*
> ¼ *cup pure maple syrup*
> ⅓ *cup coarsely chopped pecans*

1. Wash and scrub yams thoroughly. Place in a 6-quart pot and cover with cold water. Add salt, cover, and bring to a boil. Reduce heat to medium-low and simmer until tender (25 to 35 minutes). Drain and set aside to cool. When cool, peel and cut into ¾-inch slices.

2. In a large, heavy-bottomed skillet over medium heat, melt butter. Add yam slices, a few at a time, and sauté until golden brown on both sides (about 5 minutes). Remove to serving platter and keep warm.

3. To skillet add maple syrup and pecans. Cook to heat through; pour over yams.

Serves 12.

SHALLOT-WATERCRESS SALAD

> 2 *large heads butter lettuce, washed and torn into bite-sized pieces*
> 1 *bunch watercress, washed, dried, and stemmed*
> ⅓ *cup oil*
> 2 *tablespoons red wine vinegar*
> *Pinch salt*
> 1 *teaspoon Dijon mustard*
> 2 *shallots, minced*

1. In a large bowl combine lettuce and watercress.

2. In a small bowl combine oil, vinegar, salt, mustard, and shallots. Whisk to blend. Toss dressing over greens and serve.

Serves 12.

CARDAMOM ROLLS

- 1 cup milk
- 2 tablespoons sugar
- 2 tablespoons butter
- ½ teaspoon salt
- 1 package dry yeast
- 2 tablespoons lukewarm (105°F to 110°F) water
- 1 egg
- 3½ cups flour
- 2 teaspoons ground cardamom
  Melted butter

1. In a small saucepan scald milk. Stir in sugar, butter, and salt. Let cool to lukewarm (105° F to 110° F).

2. In a large bowl sprinkle yeast over water; add lukewarm milk mixture and egg and stir to mix well.

3. Sift flour with cardamom. Gradually add flour to liquid, stirring with a wooden spoon. Knead in flour when dough is too stiff to stir.

4. Place dough in a buttered bowl and turn dough to coat thoroughly with butter. Cover with a clean cloth and let rise in a warm place until doubled in bulk, about 1½ hours.

5. Punch dough down; shape into 2-inch balls. Arrange on baking sheet. Flatten dough balls slightly with palm of hand. Cover with a cloth and let rise again until doubled in bulk (about 1 hour). While dough rises, preheat oven to 425° F.

6. Bake rolls in center of middle rack of oven until golden brown (12 to 15 minutes). Brush with melted butter and serve.

Makes 12 dinner rolls.

TRIFLE

Génoise

- ⅔ cup all-purpose flour
- ⅓ cup cake flour
- ½ cup unsalted butter
- 4 eggs, at room temperature
- ⅔ cup sugar
- 2 teaspoons vanilla extract

Custard

- 2 cups milk
- ¼ cup cornstarch
- ¼ teaspoon salt
- ⅔ cup sugar
- 3 egg yolks
- 2 teaspoons vanilla extract
- 1 cup whipping cream

Filling

- 2 cups fresh or frozen (thawed) raspberries
- 2 tablespoons rum

Topping

- 1 cup whipping cream, beaten until stiff

1. *To prepare génoise:* Preheat oven to 375° F. Line a 12- by 16-inch jelly roll pan with waxed paper, letting it extend at least 1 inch above all pan sides. Generously grease waxed paper.

2. Onto a large square of waxed paper, sift flours together; set aside. In small saucepan over low heat, melt butter; set aside.

3. In large bowl of electric mixer at slow speed, beat eggs. Gradually add sugar, then vanilla. Beat at high speed until eggs have doubled in volume and are lemon colored. Sift one third of the flour over batter, folding quickly with a spatula. Then add flour alternately with melted butter, folding quickly until all the flour and butter are incorporated.

4. Spread batter evenly in jelly roll pan. Bake in center of middle rack of oven until lightly golden (12 to 15 minutes).

5. Remove cake from pan. When it is cool, invert onto a cutting board and peel away waxed paper. Cut cake into 1- by 4-inch strips; set aside.

6. *To prepare custard:* Scald 1½ cups of the milk. In a medium saucepan combine cornstarch, salt, sugar, and remaining milk. Gradually stir in scalded milk. Bring to a boil over medium-high heat, stirring constantly. Reduce heat to medium-low and continue cooking until thickened (about 3 minutes). Beat in egg yolks and cook 2 minutes. Add vanilla. Cover and chill about 2 hours in refrigerator. (Or put the pan in a bowl of ice for about 40 minutes; stir occasionally.) Beat whipping cream until stiff. Fold into chilled mixture and refrigerate until ready to use.

7. *To prepare filling:* Combine raspberries and rum. Refrigerate until ready to use.

8. *To assemble:* Line a 4-quart soufflé dish with strips of génoise. Cover with a layer of raspberry-rum mixture and a layer of custard. Continue layering until all cake, raspberries, and custard are used, ending with custard. *To serve:* Spoon trifle onto dessert plates and top with a dollop of whipped cream.

Serves 12.

CHOCOLATE TRUFFLES

- 6 ounces semisweet chocolate
- ½ cup unsalted butter, cut in 8 pieces
- ¼ cup whipping cream
- 1 cup confectioners' sugar
- 2 teaspoons orange-flavored liqueur
- ¼ cup cocoa powder

1. In a double boiler melt chocolate over simmering water. Stir butter into melted chocolate, a piece at a time. Slowly pour in cream, stirring constantly. Remove from heat.

2. Gradually sift in confectioners' sugar, stirring rapidly until smooth. Stir in liqueur. Cover and refrigerate for at least 12 hours.

3. Sift cocoa onto a plate. Scoop up chocolate in teaspoonfuls. With hands, shape chocolate into ¾-inch balls (chocolate will melt a bit when handled). Roll in cocoa and set on another plate. Store, covered, in refrigerator until ready to serve.

Makes about 2 dozen truffles.

Leftovers can be glamorous, as demonstrated by Chinese Duck Salad, served cold on a bed of shredded lettuce and puffy fried rice vermicelli.

LEFTOVERS: A BOON, NOT A BURDEN

Leftovers unfairly suffer second-class status. Instead of being scorned as the recycled remains of yesterday's dinner, they should be lauded as a convenience to the cook. When handled with creativity and imagination, leftovers can be the starting point for any number of original and delicious meals—and because they are already cooked, they make meal preparation a streamlined process.

Keep in mind also that leftover poultry needn't be used immediately. Properly packaged for storage, cooked meat can be kept in the refrigerator for up to a week and in the freezer for up to two months.

CHINESE DUCK SALAD

Make this salad to use up the duck legs left over from Broiled Duck Breasts (see page 48). To toast almonds, cook in a small dry skillet over medium-high heat, stirring with a spoon, until golden brown (about 5 minutes).

> 4   cups Duck or Chicken Stock (see page 91)
> 4   duck legs, washed and patted dry
> ½   cup soy sauce
> 1   tablespoon minced fresh ginger
> 1   clove garlic, minced
> 2   cups vegetable oil
> 3   ounces rice vermicelli
> 1   head iceberg lettuce, washed and shredded
> 2   green onions, thinly sliced
> ½   cup toasted slivered almonds

Soy Dressing

> 1   cup oil
> ¾   cup rice wine vinegar
> ½   cup sugar
> 2   tablespoons soy sauce

1. In a large, heavy-bottomed skillet, bring stock to a boil. Add duck legs, cover, and return to a boil. Reduce heat to medium-low and simmer, covered, until cooked (about 25 minutes). Remove duck legs and cool completely. When cool, remove skin and discard. Tear meat off bones and cut into small cubes.

2. In a medium bowl combine soy sauce, ginger, and garlic. Add duck meat and toss to coat. Cover and refrigerate 8 to 24 hours.

3. When ready to assemble salad, heat oil in wok to 365° F (measure with a deep-fat thermometer). Fry rice vermicelli, a handful at a time, until it puffs (about 30 to 60 seconds). Be careful not to let it brown. Remove with slotted spoon and drain on paper towel. Set aside.

4. Place lettuce in a large bowl. Remove duck from marinade with slotted spoon, drain, and pat dry. Toss with lettuce, green onions, and almonds. Toss with Soy Dressing and serve surrounded with rice vermicelli.

Serves 4.

Soy Dressing In a small bowl whisk together oil, vinegar, sugar, and soy sauce.

Makes about 2¼ cups.

HOT CHICKEN SALAD

This familiar and homey baked casserole incorporates ingredients that are typically part of a cold chicken salad. You can make it with leftover cooked chicken, or follow the subrecipe to prepare a chicken especially for this dish.

> *3 cups diced cooked chicken (or make Chicken for Salad, below)*
> *½ cup Mayonnaise (see page 107)*
> *Half an onion, minced*
> *½ cup whole almonds*
> *¾ cup grated sharp Cheddar cheese*

Chicken for Salad

> *1 frying chicken (about 3 lbs)*
> *2 medium carrots, peeled and cut in 2-inch pieces*
> *2 stalks celery, cut in 2-inch pieces*
> *1 large onion, quartered*
> *2 sprigs parsley*

1. If necessary, prepare Chicken for Salad.

2. Preheat oven to 350° F. In a medium bowl combine chicken, mayonnaise, minced onion, and whole almonds. Turn mixture into a 2-quart casserole; top with grated cheese.

3. Bake until bubbly and heated through (about 30 minutes). Serve immediately.

Serves 4 to 6.

Chicken for Salad

1. Wash chicken; remove innards and excess fat. Put chicken in a stockpot or Dutch oven. Add carrots, celery, quartered onion, and parsley. Add enough cold water to cover.

2. Bring to a boil, partially covered. Skim off any scum that may have risen to the surface. Reduce heat to medium-low and simmer gently, covered, until bird is just tender when pierced with a fork (about 25 minutes).

3. Remove bird from pot and set aside to cool. Strain broth and save for another use. When chicken is cool, remove meat from bones and cut into ⅛-inch dice.

MEXICAN TURKEY CASSEROLE

The Mexican seasonings in this casserole offer a nice change from the flavors that are usually partnered with turkey.

> *3 tablespoons butter*
> *3 tablespoons flour*
> *1 cup Chicken Stock (see page 91)*
> *1 cup whipping cream*
> *1 small onion, minced*
> *1 can (4 oz) mild green chiles, diced*
> *1 jar (8 oz) salsa*
> *10 corn tortillas, cut in 2-inch strips*
> *4 cups cubed cooked turkey*
> *½ pound Cheddar cheese, grated*
> *1 cup sour cream*

1. Preheat oven to 350° F. Butter a 1½-quart casserole.

2. In a medium, heavy-bottomed skillet over medium-high heat, melt butter. Add flour, stirring constantly to blend. Cook about 2 minutes. Slowly add Chicken Stock, whisking constantly. Add cream, whisking constantly. Remove from heat and set aside.

3. In a small bowl mix together onion, chiles, and salsa; set aside.

4. Make a layer of tortilla strips in casserole. Top with layers of turkey, sauce, salsa mixture, and cheese. Repeat layers until all ingredients are used, ending with cheese.

5. Bake in center of middle rack of oven until golden brown and bubbling (about 40 minutes). Serve with dollops of sour cream.

Serves 6.

CALIFORNIA PITA WITH HERB SPREAD

For many turkey lovers, turkey sandwiches with mayonnaise are as much of a treat as the roasted bird itself. Here's a sandwich with a California flavor, using an herbed spread.

> *2 tablespoons mayonnaise*
> *2 tablespoons sour cream*
> *¼ teaspoon snipped fresh dill or 1 teaspoon dried*
> *1 large clove garlic, crushed*
> *4 pieces whole wheat pita bread, halved*
> *½ pound cooked chicken or turkey, thinly sliced*
> *4 radishes, washed and thinly sliced*
> *Half a ripe avocado, peeled, pitted, and cubed*
> *Sprouts*

1. In a small bowl combine mayonnaise, sour cream, dill, and garlic.

2. In each pita half place an equal amount of chicken, herb spread, radishes, avocado, and sprouts. Serve.

Makes 8 sandwiches.

CROQUE MADAME

This well-known grilled sandwich is wonderfully simple. It is especially attractive if you use a toasting iron to impress a shell pattern on the bread.

> 8 thin slices white sandwich bread
> 8 slices Emmenthaler cheese (about 8 oz)
> ½ pound cooked chicken
> ½ cup butter

1. On a slice of bread, layer 1 slice cheese, one fourth of the chicken, and another slice of cheese. Cover with a slice of bread. Repeat with remaining bread and filling.

2. In a large sauté pan or skillet over medium-high heat, melt butter. Reduce heat to medium and add sandwiches; sauté until golden brown on both sides (about 4 to 5 minutes per side). Drain on paper towels. Slice and serve.

Makes 4 sandwiches.

TURKEY-CRANBERRY SANDWICHES

The addition of orange rind to the biscuit dough makes a nice complement to the turkey and cranberry sauce. Serve these bite-sized sandwiches at a brunch or as a light supper with some cold salads.

> ½ cup fresh or canned cranberry sauce
> ½ pound cooked turkey, thinly sliced

Orange Biscuits

> 1½ cups flour
> 1 tablespoon baking powder
> 1 teaspoon sugar
> ½ teaspoon salt
> Grated rind of 1 medium orange (about 2 tablespoons)
> 2 tablespoons butter, chilled
> 1 tablespoon cold vegetable shortening
> ½ cup milk mixed with 1 egg yolk
> Milk or melted butter for glaze

Prepare Orange Biscuits. Split biscuits in half. On each of 8 biscuit halves, spread 2 tablespoons cranberry sauce; top with turkey. Cover with remaining biscuit halves.

Makes 8 sandwiches.

Orange Biscuits

1. Preheat oven to 425° F. In a medium bowl sift together flour, baking powder, sugar, and salt; mix in orange rind. Cut butter and shortening into flour with a pastry blender or two knives. Make a well in center of dough. Pour milk-egg mixture into well, stirring with a wooden spoon until mixed.

2. Turn dough onto a lightly floured board. Knead gently 8 to 10 times. Roll out dough ¼ to ½ inch thick. Cut with a biscuit cutter or inverted glass (3 inches in diameter).

3. Place on an ungreased cookie sheet. Bake until golden brown (12 to 15 minutes). When done, brush with milk or melted butter.

Makes 8 biscuits.

PÂTÉS AND TERRINES

Perhaps no other food demonstrates the inventiveness and artistry of cooking more than pâtés and terrines. These elegant appetizers and first courses—much like the American meat loaf, but with a richer, more luxurious texture and flavor—probably developed as a Gallic solution to the universal problem of leftovers.

A pâté is a spreadable paste of ground meats, livers, and seasonings. Its consistency can be airy and smooth, like a mousse, or more coarsely textured and country style. Ingredients for pâtés can be precooked and then combined, or the mixture can be processed and then baked in a crust or in a mold, which is often lined with pork fat. Special containers called terrine molds are traditionally used for pâtés, but any loaf pan of equal volume will work just as well.

Pâtés are easy to prepare, especially with a food processor, although they may require costly or hard-to-find ingredients. They're wonderful for entertaining because they improve when aged for several days in the refrigerator.

Plan ahead for the chicken-liver pâtés below by freezing chicken livers when cleaning fresh whole birds. Two cups of livers (1 pound) will make one pâté recipe. They will be ready to serve after chilling in the refrigerator; the Pâté Maison needs two to three days of refrigeration.

PÂTÉ MAISON

> 2 tablespoons butter
> Half a medium onion, minced
> ½ cup plus 2 tablespoons Cognac
> 1 pound ground pork
> 1 pound ground veal
> 1 clove garlic, minced
> 2 eggs, slightly beaten
> 1 teaspoon salt
> ⅛ teaspoon pepper
> 1 teaspoon dried thyme
> 1 chicken breast, boned and skinned
> 1 pound pork fat, cut into ⅛-inch slices
> 2 ounces pistachio nuts, shelled

1. Preheat oven to 350° F. In a small skillet over medium heat, melt butter until it foams. Add onions and sauté over medium-high heat until translucent. Pour in ½ cup of the Cognac. Cook until Cognac is absorbed into onions (mixture will measure about ⅓ cup). Remove from heat and place in a large mixing bowl.

2. Add pork, veal, garlic, eggs, salt, pepper, and thyme. Mix with hands until thoroughly blended, or blend in food processor until light in texture and well blended.

3. Cut chicken breast into ½- by 3-inch slices. Put slices in a small bowl and add the remaining 2 tablespoons Cognac.

4. Line a 2-quart terrine or loaf pan with slices of pork fat. Press one half of ground-meat mixture into pan. Cover with Cognac-soaked chicken and then pistachios. Press remaining ground-meat mixture on top. Cover with another layer of pork fat.

5. Cover terrine with aluminum foil. Set in a pan of boiling water. Place on rack in center of oven. Bake until juices run clear yellow and pâté has shrunk from sides of pan.

6. When pâté is done, remove terrine and set on cooling rack. Place another loaf pan on top of pâté; fill with 3 to 4 pounds of weight (canned goods or bricks work well). Let pâté cool at room temperature for several hours, then refrigerate 2 to 3 days before slicing. To serve, unmold and slice.

Serves 10 as a first course.

CHOPPED CHICKEN LIVERS

> 2 tablespoons olive oil
> 2 large onions, sliced
> 1 pound chicken livers, washed, dried, and trimmed
> 4 hard-cooked eggs, peeled and cooled (see page 7)
> ¼ cup Mayonnaise (see page 107)
> Salt and freshly ground black pepper

1. In a large skillet heat oil. Add onions and sauté until golden brown (about 7 minutes). Add chicken livers and cook over medium-high heat until golden brown on outside but still pink on inside (about 5 minutes). Remove from flame and allow to cool.

2. In a blender or food processor, process liver-onion mixture with eggs (keep mixture a little lumpy). Pour into a medium bowl. Stir in Mayonnaise. Season with salt and pepper. Chill thoroughly before serving.

Makes 2 cups.

CHICKEN LIVER PÂTÉ

> ¼ cup butter
> 2 shallots, peeled and sliced
> ½ teaspoon dried thyme
> 1 pound chicken livers, washed, dried, and trimmed
> 2 tablespoons each Cognac and whipping cream
> Salt and freshly ground black pepper

1. In a medium skillet heat butter until it foams. Add shallots and thyme. Sauté until shallots are golden brown (4 to 5 minutes). Add chicken livers and cook over medium-high heat until golden brown on outside but still pink within (about 5 minutes).

2. In a blender or food processor, purée livers until smooth. Turn into a bowl. Stir in Cognac and cream. Season with salt and pepper. Chill thoroughly before serving.

Makes 2 cups.

The sometimes neglected chicken liver can be transformed into a smooth and velvety pâté. Petite cornichons and crusty French bread are traditional accompaniments.

U.S. MEASURE AND METRIC MEASURE CONVERSION CHART

Formulas for Exact Measures	Symbol	When you know:	Multiply by:	To find:	**Rounded Measures for Quick Reference**		
Mass (Weight)	oz	ounces	28.35	grams	1 oz		= 30 g
	lb	pounds	0.45	kilograms	4 oz		= 115 g
	g	grams	0.035	ounces	8 oz		= 225 g
	kg	kilograms	2.2	pounds	16 oz	= 1 lb	= 450 g
					32 oz	= 2 lb	= 900 g
					36 oz	= 2¼ lb	= 1,000 g (1 kg)
Volume	tsp	teaspoons	5.0	milliliters	¼ tsp	= 1/24 oz	= 1 ml
	tbsp	tablespoons	15.0	milliliters	½ tsp	= 1/12 oz	= 2 ml
	fl oz	fluid ounces	29.57	milliliters	1 tsp	= 1/6 oz	= 5 ml
	c	cups	0.24	liters	1 tbsp	= ½ oz	= 15 ml
	pt	pints	0.47	liters	1 c	= 8 oz	= 250 ml
	qt	quarts	0.95	liters	2 c (1 pt)	= 16 oz	= 500 ml
	gal	gallons	3.785	liters	4 c (1 qt)	= 32 oz	= 1 l.
	ml	milliliters	0.034	fluid ounces	4 qt (1 gal)	= 128 oz	= 3¾ l.
Length	in.	inches	2.54	centimeters	⅜ in.	= 1 cm	
	ft	feet	30.48	centimeters	1 in.	= 2.5 cm	
	yd	yards	0.9144	meters	2 in.	= 5 cm	
	mi	miles	1.609	kilometers	2½ in.	= 6.5 cm	
	km	kilometers	0.621	miles	12 in. (1 ft)	= 30 cm	
	m	meters	1.094	yards	1 yd	= 90 cm	
	cm	centimeters	0.39	inches	100 ft	= 30 m	
					1 mi	= 1.6 km	
Temperature	° F	Fahrenheit	5/9 (after subtracting 32)	Celsius	32° F	= 0° C	
					68° F	= 20° C	
	° C	Celsius	9/5 (then add 32)	Fahrenheit	212° F	= 100° C	
Area	in.^{2}	square inches	6.452	square centimeters	1 in.^{2}	= 6.5 cm^2	
	ft^2	square feet	929.0	square centimeters	1 ft^2	= 930 cm^2	
	yd^2	square yards	8,361.0	square centimeters	1 yd^2	= 8,360 cm^2	
	a	acres	0.4047	hectares	1 a	= 4,050 m^2	

Special Thanks To:

Bill Hughes
John A. Brown Kitchenwares
Oakland, CA

Ann Lyman
Feather River Wood Products
Piedmont, CA

Tim Magnani
Magnani's Poultry
Oakland, CA

Denis C. Spanek
Spanek—The Creative Cookware Co.
San Mateo, CA

Dr. George York
University of California Cooperative Extension
Davis, CA

Leila and Simon Childs
Ken and Toni Hastings
Andrew Mayer
Sharon Parker
Ken and Janet Wolfe

and the following, all of San Francisco, CA:

Antique Center
Argentum Antiques Ltd.
Biordi Italian Imports
Claire's Linens
Clervi Marble
Decor Galleries
Fillamento
Forrest Jones
La Tienda, The Mexican Museum
La Ville du Soleil
New Castle Architectural Antiques
Paul Bauer Inc.
Pierre Deux Original Fabrics
Rushcutters
Set Your Table
Silk Route
Tiffany & Co.
Wedgwood
William B. Meyer Silver
Williams-Sonoma